3 0063 00240 0952

W9-BYW-789

Let it Go

Let it Go

Downsizing Your Way to a
RICHER, HAPPIER LIFE

PETER WALSH
NEW YORK TIMES BESTSELLING AUTHOR

RODALE.

RODALE
wellness

Live happy. Be healthy. Get inspired.

Sign up today to get exclusive access to our authors,
exclusive bonuses, and the most authoritative, useful, and
cutting-edge information on health, wellness, fitness,
and living your life to the fullest.

Visit us online at RodaleWellness.com
Join us at RodaleWellness.com/Join

Internet addresses and telephone numbers given in this book were accurate at the time it went to press.

© 2017 by Peter Walsh

Simultaneously published in hardcover by Pan Macmillan Australia

Rodale books may be purchased for business or promotional use or for special sales. For information, please write to: Special Markets Department, Rodale Inc., 733 Third Avenue, New York, NY 10017.

Printed in the United States of America

Rodale Inc. makes every effort to use acid-free ♾, recycled paper ♻.

Book design by Christina Gaugler

Library of Congress Cataloging-in-Publication Data is on file with the publisher.

ISBN-13: 978–1–62336–779–4 hardcover

Distributed to the trade by Macmillan

2   4   6   8   10   9   7   5   3   1   hardcover

Follow us @RodaleBooks on

We inspire health, healing, happiness, and love in the world.
Starting with you.

To my family and friends, who taught me when something's important enough to hold on to... and when I need to let it go.

CONTENTS

INTRODUCTION

Welcome to an experience that could be one of the most rewarding times of your life.

Don't believe me? I understand. You've probably gotten the impression that downsizing should be a fear-inducing task. Honestly, how could it *not* be?

As you travel through life, you encounter milestones that require you to comb through the stuff you've gathered: relocating to a new city; getting married and combining homes with another person; hitting tough times that send you into a smaller home; kids growing up and leaving the family home empty (and unnecessarily large); or the death of a spouse or parent.

When you downsize for these changes, you're likely to confront some of life's deepest questions. That's one reason why the process is so often painful. Downsizing requires us to confront our insecurities, our relationships, and our own mortality. The stuff you sift through has the power to evoke deep emotions and memories, which can easily derail you.

Downsizing can require you to shrink a houseful of possessions so they'll fit into a new space that may be much smaller than what you have now. Many of these possessions are things you *really, really* like. They're probably things you couldn't *possibly* live without! To make the mission even more challenging, you're likely working on an uncomfortably tight deadline.

Sound familiar?

Or maybe you're facing another common type of downsizing

scenario: the task of wading through a lifetime of items that belonged to someone else, like your parents, grandparents, or other loved ones. Their home contains stuff that might be important to you . . . but you probably have even less time to manage this kind of downsizing.

Sound familiar?

While standing on the brink of a downsizing project, you might be terrified that you'll make a bad decision, throw out the wrong thing, alienate your family, infuriate your parents, or just disappear into an abyss of clutter and never be seen or heard from again!

Sound familiar?

It does to me. The challenge of downsizing the possessions in a home—whether their own or someone else's—petrifies many people. I know this well, because I've helped thousands deal with the clutter in their homes. Thousands more have asked for guidance on what to keep and what to let go while moving or downsizing. I've also had to downsize under trying circumstances that faced my own family.

My mother cared for my father for years during his long illness. Four years after he passed away, her failing health brought her to an assisted living facility. Old age and steadily advancing dementia made her last few years difficult, and then, hard as it was to believe, she was gone, too.

My younger sister, Julie, and I stood outside the facility on a chilly Australian day just after her passing. We were there to clean out her room. Of the few possessions Mum still owned, we donated most to a local charity. The rest fit into the two boxes Julie and I clutched in the cold.

She turned to me and asked, "Mum lived for 92 years, and here each of us is carrying a cardboard box. Is this the sum of her life?"

Those boxes held the last few treasures that were important

to my mother, Kath, at the very end of her exceptional life. Growing up in a poor farming family, she didn't complete the 8th grade. Instead, she left home at 14 and traveled hundreds of miles across Australia to train as a nurse. A few years later, caring for wounded soldiers would be her contribution during World War II.

By the time she was 34, she had 5 children under the age of 7 and would go on to add 2 more kids to our family. My siblings raised 12 children of their own, who all became successful, well-educated professionals.

My sister and I kept only our mother's hairbrush, rosary beads, photos, and notes she had jotted down about her family to jog her memory.

That was it. These few things were the last of the mementos that could represent our mother. All the other objects that she had touched and used during her life had been distributed long ago.

I finally found the words to respond to Julie's question. "Mum's life was not about the *stuff*," I said. What made her life shine had nothing to do with any of the objects she owned. Whether she held on to it for a minute or 90 years, her stuff was ultimately finite and temporary.

The intangible things Mum left behind—her laugh, her wicked sense of humor, and her wise advice—will live on. In the following days and months, my siblings and I would take great joy in understanding her legacy: her children, grandchildren, and great-grandchildren. Amazing stories from old friends at the funeral service. A flood of wonderful cards and condolences. And quiet snippets of conversation that revealed so much about the goodness and kindness of the amazing woman who was my mother.

Earlier, when we were downsizing my parents' home, one of

the few things I kept was a green glass pie plate she used for making desserts when we were children. Our now-scattered family once gathered around this plate. Our mother's hands held this plate. Her serving spoon left a few scratches on its surface as she fed us and adored us.

This object is so much more than a plate. For me, it's a truly treasured possession.

I'm telling you this so that you don't think my advice for downsizing will be simply to discard everything! The amount I kept worked for me, and I'll help you find the amount that works for you.

I know why so many people think downsizing is scary. But I can promise you that if you do it correctly, the process won't live up to the disruptive, divisive, and stressful reputation it's gotten.

Many people, feeling overwhelmed, have come to me looking for a system that solves their downsizing dilemma.

Here it is.

The *Let It Go* way of downsizing makes the process logical, manageable, and as swift as possible. This method provides solutions to the pressure and turmoil you may feel when you trim down your belongings or your loved ones'.

The *Let It Go* method also corrects the wrong impressions about downsizing that you may have learned! I'll lead you step-by-step through a *different* sort of downsizing process, one that prepares you emotionally and mentally beforehand, then helps you rapidly sift through your pile of stuff and discover benefits that others rarely find, like:

- New insights into the memories you've made and the relationships you've had over your life, which you'll discover while examining the keepsakes linked to these memories and relationships

- Better communication with your loved ones who are going through the downsizing process with you

- More happiness, focus, and confidence as you head into this next phase in your life

DOWNSIZING IS A NORMAL— AND NECESSARY—PART OF LIFE

Most homes are filled with items that represent a lifetime's worth of adventures and accomplishments. Some of this stuff is truly necessary. Much isn't.

You have cookware and bedding to help you eat and sleep. Your books, magazines, and electronics entertain you. Your computers, woodworking tools, and musical instruments help you create. Your clothes, cars, and jewelry inform the world about the status you've achieved or hope to attain.

But as you travel from one stage of your life into another, sometimes you need to shift direction or venture through circumstances that are a little more cramped. Your new reality means that you won't be able to comfortably bring all your possessions with you.

Or maybe a parent has died or needs to move into a smaller home, and you have to sort through family possessions and decide what to keep. As you'll see in several people's stories later, keeping too much can put your happiness at risk.

To move forward, you have three choices:

- You can stress yourself mentally and physically by trying to bring along stuff that no longer fits in your life or space.

- You can do the typical kind of downsizing that people dread, quickly speeding through it while giving it as little thought as possible. This often leads to later regrets.

■ You can downsize in a way that gives you peace of mind and helps you enjoy the next stage of your life to the maximum. This is the *Let It Go* way.

PEOPLE NEED A BETTER WAY TO DOWNSIZE

Downsizing isn't just a spring cleaning. It's far more than a casual decluttering project. Instead, it requires you to *seriously* inspect your stuff and offload a large portion of it. Chances are that you'll only go through a downsizing project a few times in your life.

This process presents a special challenge because you're already struggling with other major changes in your life. The distress of parting with stuff can be an ordeal on its own. But you're probably also confronting painful memories and uncomfortable realizations during this time: "I'm grieving over the loss of a loved one," or "How will I get by on less income?" Just in case that weren't enough, you may be trying to sell a home, buy a new place, and schedule the moving trucks, too.

The *Let It Go* way helps you efficiently make the right decisions about your possessions, even if you're feeling these hardships. I'll cover the common downsizing difficulties that people face, and I'll help you apply the techniques and methods I've developed to your specific challenges.

It starts with this central idea: As you look around the rooms filled with the stuff you have to process, the hurt or confusion you feel about getting rid of some of it is not about the stuff. You're only seeing the surface level. You have to dig deeper. Way down, underneath all this clutter, is where you confront the idea that:

■ **You are not your stuff** or your bank account, either, or even your career. If you've defined yourself by what you own or what you do for a living (don't feel bad—a lot of people do this!), downsizing requires you to examine your way of thinking.

■ **You're entering a new phase** that will change your identity. The milestone that has prompted your downsizing is an announcement that you're no longer a child, a single person, a married person, a career worker, the owner of a big house in a prestigious neighborhood, a person who can call home and talk to mom and dad, or whomever you were before the downsizing event.

■ **Many items you need to shed** are firmly glued to you with a sticky layer of memories, sadness, anxiety, and guilt.

■ **Family tension** may arise as soon as you start talking about shedding possessions.

Sometimes our attachments to our stuff become overwhelming and paralyzing. In my experience, when you get to this point, your ability to make decisions becomes impaired. Focused action becomes nearly impossible.

When you can't let your stuff go, your stuff won't let you move forward.

LIGHTEN YOUR LOAD AND GET OUT OF YOUR RUT

I've worked with people who filled a storage unit with the entire contents of grandma's house after she died. Twenty years later, they were still paying rent on that unit but not once had they looked at the stuff inside. Some people may fill their own homes with a departed relative's memories. Or they still hang on to their kids' childhoods after these sons and daughters have started their own families.

Your physical possessions—and the emotional weight they carry—can become so heavy that your wheels sink under the load. Even if you move into a new stage of your life, you can't appreciate it fully because you're crushed under your old stuff.

When you downsize well, you will emerge lighter and liberated. You will be surrounded only by items that bring you joy and pleasure. You're able to make the most of your new opportunities.

Rest assured that you won't simply wipe your slate clean of all your treasured possessions and walk away empty-handed. That's not the *Let It Go* way. If you simply jettison your possessions without confronting the deeper issues attached to the objects, you'll still have all your old traumas, and all your sadness and anxiety and guilt. You'll still have unresolved family conflicts and disappointments. All these invisible burdens will come with you. They'll hamper you from enjoying the next stage of your life (and you'll just buy new stuff to conceal them).

So what is the *Let It Go* way? You'll purposefully confront the items now filling your home. Which ones bring up bad memories? Which ones are creating a wall around you that will keep you from grabbing the new prospects your life is about to offer?

Also, which possessions represent the legacy of your loved ones that you want to preserve? Which possessions can someday carry on your legacy?

Likely, this process will involve some of your loved ones—perhaps your children, whether they're young or grown; your spouse; your siblings; or your parents. The *Let It Go* way of downsizing presents an amazing opportunity to resolve problems, strengthen connections, and rediscover meaning in these relationships.

This kind of downsizing does take work. It also takes time. I understand that you may already feel frazzled and overscheduled, with little desire to take on more challenges. But using this approach can actually make downsizing faster and easier. And it's going to make the next phase of your life so much better.

In recent years, I've dealt with several of life's big milestones. And I have more coming in the near future.

As I write this, my husband and I are contemplating moving to a smaller home in another city, which will require us to let some of our possessions go. I've also reached an age (I'll keep the specific number to myself, thanks) that allows me to see that the busiest phase of my working life will someday come to an end. It's not anytime soon . . . but it's not the hypothetical scenario it was when I was 30.

Here's what I have discovered, both from my own life and from so many other people's stories. These milestones that mark a new transition can shake you to your core. They can leave you wondering what you did with your life and worrying about what comes next. "Have I made the right decisions so far? Am I making the right decision now?" you might ask.

But with these challenges comes a great opportunity to start anew—if you'll just let yourself do it.

Releasing your possessions can be terrifying, because without them, who are you? When you do it well, downsizing will answer that question.

It will also provide many other gifts. One of these is *relief*. But too many people miss it because they're squabbling with a sibling over a doll collection that neither really wants. Another gift of downsizing correctly is *freedom*. But too many people overlook it because they're frantically loading a moving truck with dusty boxes that they'll put directly into the attic of their next home.

Your life is changing, and you may or may not have asked for these changes.

But you now have the greatest opportunity that you will ever get to create the life you want. I want to help you make the most of it.

Ready to let go? Then let's go!

The Powerful Benefits of Downsizing

Though many people have little trouble finding a reason to buy *more, more, more* stuff, marketers are always happy to give them another excuse to pull out their credit cards.

Consumers in China have embraced a new holiday: Singles' Day, a celebration for people not in relationships, which falls on November 11. In one recent year, the nation's equivalent of Amazon.com sold more than $14 *billion* worth of stuff on this day.

If Singles' Day catches on in America and elsewhere in the near future, I wouldn't be surprised in the least. On the other hand, enough people are now seeing the value in a simpler lifestyle that puts less emphasis on stuff that I could also see a different type of holiday catching on: Downsizing Day!

We often stockpile stuff because that's what society has taught us to do. Some of this stuff has "heirloom" status because our parents, grandparents, or an uncle whose name we don't remember told us long ago that we needed to value it.

As you approach your own Downsizing Day, it's time for *you* to take control of these decisions. Instead of buying *new* stuff you don't need, you'll let go of *existing* stuff you don't need. Before you begin, I'd like for you to explore the big questions in this section:

- Why should I let go of my stuff?
- If I do let it go, am I ready to discover the real "me" underneath it?

CHAPTER 1

A Nation Looks for a Place to Put Its Treasures

At the moment, I'm looking at a piece of furniture on Craigslist that's less than 10 years old but already looks like a relic of a long-gone, whimsically quaint era.

It's a Mission-style oak entertainment center. At 12 feet wide and more than 6 feet tall, it entirely fills one wall of a living room. Its owner, who is trying to sell it for a fraction of what it must have cost, says it's "solidly built" and "will last several lifetimes."

I definitely believe it's solidly built. But I'm skeptical about this "several lifetimes" part. I doubt many people would want this piece of furniture *today*, let alone 50 years from now! It was created to hold a massive, boxy television on its pedestal-like stand. Mighty towers at either side contain slide-out shelves to display CDs and DVDs. Remember those?

Backbreaking armoires and entertainment centers like this had their time in American homes, and that time was brief. Shortly after they became common in living rooms and family rooms, the technology they were designed to display began vanishing.

Flat-screen TVs became thin enough to hang from a wall like artwork. Dust-collecting stacks of CDs gave way to digital music that is stored on a smartphone. By streaming movies and TV shows over your home's Wi-Fi signal, you can now live a fully entertained life without a DVD player.

As I write this, 311 other people in the Los Angeles area are also trying to unload their oak entertainment centers and armoires. Across the country, these things loiter on curbs holding "For Sale" signs (or "Free" signs), stand side-by-side in thrift stores and donation centers, and lurk in basements where

HOUSEHOLD TREASURES CAN GROW OUTDATED SURPRISINGLY QUICKLY

If you want proof that our tastes change faster than our stuff, consider this: Even *televisions* seem unnecessary to many young people.

According to research from Deloitte, the 14-to-25-year-old age group spent just 43 percent of their television time looking at an actual TV in 2015. Instead, they watched a computer, tablet, or smartphone for most of their time.

Of course, plenty of TV viewers and video gamers still feel there's no substitute for a 60-inch screen attached to floor-shaking speakers.

But often, people now want the flexibility of watching their shows on a portable device in the setting of their choice rather than having to report for duty in front of a big, unmovable screen.

Others don't want to buy a costly piece of equipment that only does one thing, when a cheaper device can provide Web access, communication, *and* TV.

It's worth asking yourself: Are any furnishings in your home worth selling now before they become outdated? If you're saving an item for your kids or grandchildren, will they find it useful— or ridiculous?

they've been repurposed as storage containers for household clutter.

A lot of these items—along with other outdated pieces of furniture—are also heading into the nation's landfills. As a *Wall Street Journal* story noted a few years ago, "Many people are making an unwelcome discovery: Their prized family heirlooms have turned into junk."

The typical household contains all sorts of objects that had their moment long ago, but now don't fit in. For example, fragile china sets and heavy, ornate picture frames may still look beautiful, but they're about as useful to today's young adults as a closetful of sky-blue one-piece leisure suits.

Especially problematic, according to the *Journal* story, is the so-called brown furniture. These are the heavy pieces made of solid wood, leather, and thick upholstery. They were built in bygone times for buyers who prized craftsmanship, gathered friends for meals in formal dining rooms, and held on to their stuff for the next generation because their kids actually needed it.

As long as you're comfortably settled in your home, you don't necessarily have to think about the space you're providing to items that have outlived their welcome. Maybe you've given your own giant hardwood TV cabinet a reprieve. After all, you can still fit a flat-screen TV into it, as long as it's not too big. Plus, things come back in style, don't they? Twenty years from now, maybe you'll be glad you kept it. Or one of your kids will want it for some reason.

Or maybe the cabinet has become part of the backdrop of your surroundings that you don't really notice. It's one of those things that's just *there*.

We all continually toss out items that we don't need without a second thought, like gum wrappers, gas receipts, and other trash. At the other end, we treasure special belongings that we might try to rescue if the house caught on fire, like photo albums or the family Bible with great-grandparents' birthdates.

But in between those extremes, a lot of stuff comes into your home that you can't so easily judge. It's somewhat valuable or useful, or you like it for some reason you can't quite describe, or it just seems like a thing that people are supposed to keep. So you make room for it. Your cabinets and shelves quietly absorb this growing mass.

Once this stuff is manufactured, it doesn't change. It's created during a certain era. For a certain purpose. For an audience that has certain expectations at that moment in time.

But our lives change. It's not just that technology becomes obsolete and new fashions come into style—our interests also shift and our values evolve. We become different people than we were 20 years ago. What do you do with all this stuff when you move to a smaller home, or even a new home of the same size that wasn't designed to flow around yesterday's furnishings?

On a similar note, how do you make the right decisions when you sort through your elderly parents' home after they move into assisted living? You'll never use your grandmother's sewing machine, but it's still worth something, right? It has memories attached to it that you're supposed to preserve, doesn't it? Shouldn't *someone* care about your father's collection of commemorative beer cans, even if that someone isn't you?

What are you supposed to do with all the hard-earned stuff that represents the full scope of your life, or perhaps even several lifetimes' worth of your family history? When you're taking a leap forward to a new home, how much of this collection should come with you? When mom and dad depart, which things do you keep to prove that they were here?

These are questions that a lot of people must soon ask. Unfortunately, the traditional method of downsizing provides very few answers.

MILLIONS HEADED FOR A DOWNSIZING IN THE NEAR FUTURE

For much of their lives, the nation's baby boomers have held an unusually powerful influence. These were the 72 million born between the mid-1940s and the mid-1960s, along with another 6 million of their peers who moved to America from other countries, like I did.

With such a large group rolling through life's milestones at the same time, their interests became America's interests. Their concerns became America's concerns. In the coming years, many boomers will be in the mood to move into a smaller home, and this migration will turn up the volume on the national conversation about downsizing.

Currently, another 240,000 boomers turn 65 every month, according to the AARP. Though many will keep working, this has traditionally been regarded as retirement age.

A recent survey found that 64 percent of retirees thought they would move at least once during retirement. Most often, they considered moving so they could live closer to family or lower their household expenses.

The survey also found that 51 percent of retirees had chosen a smaller home during their previous move. This all suggests that in the coming years, millions of boomers will need to shed some of their possessions to fit into a smaller place. Plenty of others who aren't currently expecting to downsize will see their plans change when they develop health or financial concerns.

Many boomers are also reaching another milestone that creates a mismatch between the mass of belongings they own compared to the space they can devote to them.

The Accenture consulting firm estimated that boomers are in the process of receiving more than $12 trillion dollars in inheritance from their parents. This is changing hands in the form of bank accounts and homes, of course, but also vehicles, artwork, and *stuff* that will need to be kept, thrown out, or sold.

Departing boomers are already starting to pass along their own possessions to their Gen X and millennial children, and

---

Woman Dreads Losing Her Stuff—And Herself—On the Eve of a Life Change

Susan Moore was having a uniquely upsetting week the first time we spoke.

A 28-foot moving truck, packed as tightly as Susan and her husband could fill it, had just pulled away from their home near San Francisco. They were in the process of loading yet *another* huge truck with their possessions. Soon Susan was going to hop into her car and drive 11 hours away to her new home near Phoenix.

"This is probably one of the hardest things I've ever had to do," Susan told me. She had lived for 31 years in the same house, where she and her husband, Rich, raised two kids. She worked as a special education teaching assistant in the elementary school she'd attended as a child. Her parents lived

three blocks away. She was "cemented and rooted" in the area, she said.

But then her family started leaving. First, her son met a local girl while attending the University of Arizona. They got married and had kids. Susan's parents visited the sunny state and soon moved there, too.

So Susan and Rich decided to follow them. Their grandkids were growing up far away, and the housing market was great for sellers but might not stay that way. "So we started working on our house, got it in tip-top shape, then listed it and sold it in 6 days," she said.

With plenty of storage space, Susan had little need over the decades to downsize her possessions. In fact, before her parents moved, "I kept going back there before they're finished, they'll leave *$30 trillion* worth of inheritance to their heirs.

This means a lot of adults—of all ages—are facing tough personal and family-related decisions:

---

and getting stuff. I have my mother's whole china set, a piece of furniture, and a couple of snow globes from her collection. I ended up with a carload, which went into the nice big shed in our backyard."

Her best friend, Nancy, who's been following my decluttering advice for years (you'll meet her on page 74), tried to talk Susan into letting go of things she didn't need. Her advice felt "brutal," Susan said.

"If it looks good, then I want to keep it. I think it's because I remember how special these things were to me before. Even if I don't use them now, I don't want to toss them. I feel like if I throw them away, I'm throwing away a piece of *me*. Everyone tells me, 'You're going on to a new chapter, so why would you want this junky stuff?' But it's not junky stuff to me," she said, emotion rising in her voice.

Susan and Rich pulled an all-nighter trying to finish clearing out their home before they had to vacate it at 8:00 a.m. Ultimately, they left a pile of useful stuff on the curb for a garbage truck to pick up, because they had no more room in their cars.

Susan was about to embark on an amazing journey, but found herself stressed out and in tears, in large part because she couldn't let her stuff go.

We made plans to reconnect later to see whether her new life would change her outlook on her possessions. Did she really need all her stuff once she got to Arizona? You'll find out at the end of the book!

- How much of my parents' stuff should I keep?
- How do I decide what's important and what's not?
- How do I want to use the next phase of my life?
- What kind of legacy do I want to leave my children?

Those downsizing in retirement or contemplating their inheritance are certainly not the only ones struggling with these kinds of decisions. People regularly hit life-changing milestones that call for downsizing throughout their adulthood, such as:

Young adults who leave the family home and start their own households. One of the first challenges for many young people who are heading out on their own is to figure out what to do with the possessions they've collected over 20-some years. (Often their parents see this as a great opportunity to sweep the family nest clean of this stuff.)

But these belongings may not fit comfortably into the apartments and houses that young adults can afford on an entry-level salary. Also, many twentysomethings don't have accurate insight into which items will be important later—which frankly is a quality they share with adults of *all* ages.

They may end up storing stuff they don't really want. (*"I can't throw this away—it was obviously important enough for mom and dad to keep for me!"*) Conversely, they may toss out childhood treasures that they'll later wish they'd kept.

Couples who are marrying and combining households. Wedging the lives of two independent young people into one home can be challenging. Second marriages that combine households with children can lead to even tougher downsizing choices. These decisions can fuel arguments at a stressful time when relationships need all the nurturing they can get. (*"How do we bring a fair amount from our old lives, while leaving room for our new family to make new memories?"*)

Couples who are divorcing and splitting their household in

two. One or both exes may need to downsize to a smaller home because of tighter finances or difficulty maintaining a large home and yard alone. (*My lawyer and I fought long and hard to keep this stuff during the divorce! Um, now what do I do with it?*)

Workers and their families who are moving long distances for a new job. Often the cost to ship a houseful of items is more than those items are actually worth! Also, relocating families may have to rent a temporary house for a while before settling into a home of their own, which means two moves loom on the horizon. (*"This job change is turning into a bigger journey than a Mars expedition!"*)

Families who must downsize because of a job loss. Though we're now years past the Great Recession, plenty of workers still face job insecurity and tight household budgets. Following a job loss, workers and their families may need to move into a smaller home and sell a lot of possessions, either because they're valuable

Real-World Downsizing Discovery

MaryLisa says: Four years ago, I moved from a traditional-style 4,000-square-foot home to an 1,800-square-foot cottage. The cottage was already fully furnished, and we knew many of our furnishings would not fit because of their size and style. I started going room by room, packing what I thought I couldn't live without and things with special meaning. I took pictures of things that I thought would be memories for my kids, but did not want to hold on to or store any longer.

I don't have a garage here, so we rented a storage unit. We now realize that there is nothing in there that justifies keeping it. Our goal is to sell or donate the contents. Thank you, Peter, for the encouragement over the years to bring us to this point.

or they won't fit. ("*This was important in our old home, but now we just can't afford to keep it.*")

Members of the military and their families. Military families normally move every 2 to 3 years. These relocations give them a regular need to decide which items to keep and which items to let go. ("*Hey, I found stuff still boxed up from our last duty station!*")

People who are heading to a home that's not smaller. Plenty of people who are moving, even retirees, have their sights set on a *bigger* home. Even if you aren't downsizing in terms of your home size, reducing the pile of stuff that goes into that home is a smart approach to take.

As you can see, the events that lead you to downsize are challenging for many reasons, not just the fact that you have to move your belongings! They often involve life-rattling changes that may only occur a few times (or, in the case of your parents' death, just once). These developments can leave you elated, exhausted, distracted, lonely, or grief-stricken.

This isn't the best state of mind for making important decisions. But there you are, having to make those decisions anyway. For many people, having to confront sorting their possessions under this emotional pressure is a uniquely stressful challenge.

That's because during the process of downsizing, several truths become obvious, sometimes painfully so:

- You own more than you really want or need—probably a *lot* more.

- Looking at your old possessions reminds you that a significant portion of your life has passed.

- Someday in the future, you'll make a move that allows you to take very little stuff, such as to a long-term care facility or, eventually, a cemetery. Downsizing reminds you that life eventually shrinks for most people. For everyone, it someday ends.

- When you die, leaving all your stuff behind, no one else will care about it like you do.

STOPPING THE CONVOY
FOR AN INSPECTION

After interviewing and surveying hundreds of older Americans, David J. Ekerdt, PhD, knows what people think about when they think about downsizing. He's the director of the University of Kansas Gerontology Center and the main researcher behind the Household Moves Project. Dr. Ekerdt is deeply involved in research that examines how people downsize, especially later in life.

He calls the massive pile of stuff that you collect and carry along your winding journey your material convoy. Picture a few moving trucks' worth of supplies that travel along with you. When you're cruising along in a spacious house with a three-car garage and shed, maybe you don't pay much attention to your convoy. But when you need to make a sudden swerve or steer your life into a smaller neighborhood, you become very aware of this load.

Some of our possessions are necessary to help us perform as "workers, partners, parents, property owners, and cultural participants," Dr. Ekerdt wrote. You buy clothes and replace them as you get older, and your body gets larger, smaller, or swings back and forth. You have kids and start buying stuff for *their* material convoys. You take up a new hobby, then

Real-World Downsizing Discovery

Patricia says: We were moving to a new city, and construction on our new house was delayed (and delayed yet again). We lived for 8 weeks in a tiny hotel suite. We only bought 2 days' worth of food at a time, and we only used the four plates, cutlery pieces, and glasses that were provided.

I soon began to question some of my possessions. Did I really need a "good" set of china, crystal glasses, and silver that were wedding gifts but that I couldn't put in the dishwasher? Did I really need to have seasonal decor items or all those boxes of books waiting for me in the storage unit? I learned to read things, pass things on to a friend or family member, or donate things. Living in small quarters with everything I *really* needed was transformational!

replace it with a newer one. You receive gifts for the ongoing cycle of holidays, birthdays, wedding anniversaries, and work anniversaries.

The society around you may pressure you to buy certain items, he said in a phone conversation. "There was this idea of femininity in decades gone by—women surrounded themselves with fine things for entertaining, like glassware, silver, crystal, and china." If they wanted to fit in, they bought this stuff. I guarantee that you feel some of this pressure, too, even if it doesn't lead to your buying a gourmet panini press.

The convoy in your home is likely to reach its peak size as you hit middle age. That's because your income tends to grow to its highest level later in your career, you may have more people living in your home, and you've simply had more time to accumulate keepsakes and gifts.

Though some items are easy to part with, shedding others can feel like losing part of *yourself*. "Our possessions are extensions of ourselves. All of these things in the convoy are part of our past selves, but they're also part of our *possible* selves. They're selves I could become, so I hang on to the object to accomplish that. All these cookbooks I have, I'm going to cook all those foods in there! I'm going to use those tools in the basement! Or the bicycle!" Dr. Ekerdt says.

These are just a few of the emotional attachments that hold objects securely in your material convoy. Your possessions also represent departed loved ones, happy times in your life, sad times that you can't stop poking at, and decisions you've made that were brilliant or unwise. They pay tribute to the joys and sorrows that occur in every life.

Of course, you have a lot of utterly useless junk mixed in there, too.

"There are objects in the convoy that we value and that are highly significant to us. But there's a lot in the convoy that we pay hardly any attention to, and there are things in the convoy that are completely mysterious to us, like those under the kitchen sink. We don't even know what they are," Dr. Ekerdt says.

When you have to separate the treasures from the trash in your material convoy, you find that it's hard physical work. It involves squatting, lifting, carrying, and sweating.

Here's another effect of downsizing that can cause an ache: Today a person who buys, consumes, and accumulates is typically viewed as a financially healthy and prized member of society. If an expanding material convoy means that you're in the prime of your career and your family life, then substantially shrinking your convoy can be unsettling. (*"Does this mean I'm becoming less useful to the world? Do my friends think less of me? Will I be less important if I own less stuff?"*)

People in the middle of a downsizing-related transition are also often moving quickly: The older people in Dr. Ekerdt's research typically had 2 months to handle the process. A quick deadline provides a convenient excuse (and a common trap) for those who don't want to do the type of thoughtful downsizing that betters their lives. (*"No time! I'll just load all these boxes into the truck and deal with them on the other end."*)

Similarly, some downsizers just delegate all the decisions to a spouse or other family member (often a daughter). Or they briskly throw stuff away without letting themselves think about what they're doing. In these cases, they may be dreading the downsizing-related milestone so much that they want to get through it as quickly as possible.

In doing so, they miss the rewards of downsizing.

At first glance, downsizing appears to be a problem of *stuff*: How do you deal with the accumulation of a lifetime (whether yours or someone else's) as painlessly as possible? Overlying this concern is often the shadow of death, family drama, or an immobilizing sense of loss and grief.

However, hidden in this process are secret gifts waiting for you, but you'll only find them if you learn how to look under these other layers of the downsizing. The new phase of your life that you're about to enter will be much poorer if you don't make a deeper inspection of the person who's steering your material convoy, who is, of course, you!

Done mindlessly or in a panicked haste, downsizing can be a gut-wrenching experience. Done well, it will lead you to a better place where you're at peace with not just your stuff, but also with your family and your life in general.

BREAK THE CYCLE AND ESCAPE
TO A BETTER PLACE

For many people, modern life in America follows the course of a big loop, with material possessions tightly intertwined with underlying emotions.

We buy things because we like the way they look, because they're a bargain, because someone recommended them, because we absolutely need them, or for no particular reason other than in that moment, we felt like it! We buy stuff because we hope it will create the life we imagine for ourselves (and how can you have a life without stuff, right?).

Much of the stuff you own represents powerful thoughts, feelings, and memories. An expert could look at the contents of your home and get a sense of what's going on inside your head. We'll meet such an expert a little later in the book. Conversely, the stuff you own—even if it's boxed up and tucked out of sight in the garage—influences how you think.

Your stuff can trigger emotions and reactions tied to a person, place, or situation. You might feel joy and happiness linked to gifts you received from someone you love. Your possessions can evoke sad feelings, too, when they remind you of an especially difficult breakup, an illness, or the death of someone you loved. Everything that you own has a place in this cycle of objects and feelings.

Let's take a look at this cycle (diagram A on the next page). The sum total of the belongings you own (in other words, the material convoy you're hauling) is the thinner black line on the outside of the diagram. This is the physical structure of your surroundings that you see every day.

Your thoughts and emotions—not only about your stuff, but about your life in general—are represented by the thicker, light-gray line within. This part is unseen and too often unexplored.

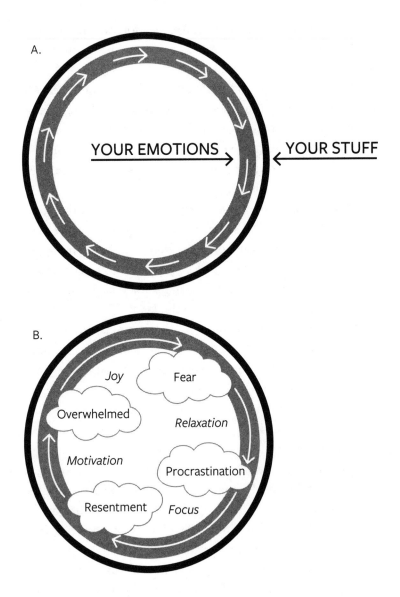

These layers of your life, comprised of the things you own and the way you feel, influence each other back and forth.

Now let's zoom in and inspect the sorts of emotions that can become tied to the things you own, sending you around and around in a cycle (diagram B). Some of these emotions are uplifting. But too often, they're quite harmful.

The negative emotions (the ones in the clouds in the diagram) have a way of appearing more noticeable in our lives, making the good feelings harder to express. If you take a moment to examine yourself, how often do you have these unpleasant emotions to some degree? Have they created just enough of a worn-down groove that they steer you away from the happiness you'd rather be enjoying?

One goal of the *Let It Go* way of downsizing is for you to surround yourself with only a manageable number of possessions that you cherish and treasure, which trigger *good* emotional responses, like joy, relaxation, focus, and motivation.

At the same time, you'll discard items that fuel the following negative emotions that can carve a rut that keeps you from your best life:

Fear. In its many forms, fear can have a powerful effect on the direction of your life. It can make you second-guess the decisions you've already made and freeze in the face of the choices you need to make now. It colors your perception of the world, so that even a turn in the road that could lead somewhere better looks scary. Also, when you scan the contents of your home, many of the objects around you are locked in place because you fear letting them go.

Procrastination. The fears you carry around can make you move slowly or not at all. You may feel unable to make decisions now, so you put them off until later. These include decisions that might lighten the burden of the possessions you're carrying. You know you're stuck, and you tell yourself that you'll deal with it "tomorrow," but, in truth, you don't know how to start moving.

Resentment. You're unhappy with some of the factors that have influenced your journey. You may feel bitter about the place you're in and the events that have brought you here. When you look at the stuff you own that tells the world "YOU ARE HERE!" you're reminded that you don't really like where "HERE" is.

Overwhelmed. These thoughts and emotions can add up to a heavy mental burden. If the pile of items around you is so heavy that it's weighing you down, or you have a lot of possessions that are tied to your mental distress, you can very understandably feel overwhelmed and paralyzed.

Finally, if you are struggling with these problems, you may be worried about what will happen next. That's the fear that starts you around the cycle again.

So now you're here in this moment. You've come upon a big transition in your life that requires you to downsize. You have a number of options. You could just launch yourself into downsizing head-on. You'd tackle the superficial layer of the stuff you see. You'd discard the items you obviously no longer want, and you'd haul away the trash. Then you'd box up the rest and take it with you.

I predict you would bring along more than the amount that would reasonably fit into your new home. Most of this excess would be stuff you don't truly want, or like, or need (or stuff you simply couldn't make a decision about). You would be starting your next phase with not only an uncomfortable amount of stuff but also the deep layer of unhappy emotions attached to it. You would arrive at an untainted, untouched new space in your life, and this is what you would unload into it.

Alternatively, you might just announce, "I'm done with it. This is all too much." You zip through your home on a slash-and-burn mission to take as little as possible and leave the past behind. You drastically reduce the physical burden you've been carrying. Essentially, you're shedding the thin outer line of the circle—the stuff—from yourself.

But you're still left with the deeper emotional layer, in which the negative aspects might still feel more prominent:

These bad feelings are like seeds you'll carry into the next phase of your life, where they can regrow.

But that's not the process I'm going to walk you through! True downsizing success comes from dealing with both layers of your life before moving forward: your stuff *and* the emotions buried beneath it.

That's the *Let It Go* way of downsizing.

Always remember that the stuff you own influences how you think. Since downsizing requires you to put your hands on items attached to deep emotions (a *lot* of items, and a *lot* of emotions), now is your best chance to adjust both. You can go from this:

To this:

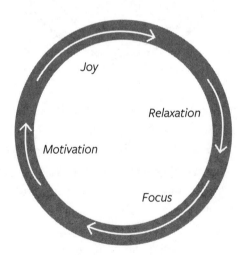

You can achieve a lighter, more open mindset that will help you better enjoy your new life. You'll also be moving forward with only two kinds of items in your material convoy: treasures that trigger very specific, happy, and significant memories that you actually want to have and functional objects that will help you thrive in your new space.

You're not bringing objects coated in negative emotions that can immediately poison your new environment. You're no longer so loaded with unwanted old memories—*"Damned if all of this stuff from Aunt Edna doesn't remind me of how I hated the mothball smell in her home!"*—that you don't have room for new memories of your choosing.

You won't be living in a shrine devoted to people who've died or a way of life that has vanished. You won't arrive at your destination feeling miserable because you brought the wrong gear, like a tourist who shows up in Thailand after packing for Sweden.

I'm excited about helping you downsize your possessions while you dig into the invisible stuff that's attached to them. It's these emotions, thoughts, and memories that change your life for better or worse. I want you to focus on these elements, then discard them, as necessary, and reframe the remaining elements of your life so they work for you.

Break open your stuff—figuratively, of course, but maybe literally, too—and inside, you'll find the gift of downsizing.

LET IT GO EXERCISE 1:
Downsizing Readiness Quiz

At the end of each of the first six chapters, I'm going to provide exercises for you to complete. I know it's a bit of extra work, but doing these will equip you with information that will make your actual downsizing faster and easier. Before you even get your moving boxes, you'll already have a good sense of what will (and will not) go into them!

For the first exercise, I'd like you to take this quick quiz to help you learn more about how you relate to your stuff, and how much excitement and/or dread you're feeling about your downsizing. Answer each question on a scale from the left (this doesn't apply to me at all) to the right (this applies to me a lot), then total your score at the end of each section. For some of the questions, the numbers are reversed due to the issue they're covering. Just answer according to how you feel from "not at all" to "very much."

Part 1: Downsizing Feelings

	NOT AT ALL				VERY MUCH	
I'm fearful about the idea of downsizing.	0	1	2	3	4	5
I'm confident that my stuff is going to fit in my new home (or my parents' stuff that I'm keeping will fit into my current home).	5	4	3	2	1	0
I'm worried that I'll make a wrong decision when downsizing.	0	1	2	3	4	5
I think downsizing will be one of the worst experiences of my life.	0	1	2	3	4	5
Downsizing will cause me a lot of emotional upheaval.	0	1	2	3	4	5
I have enough time to handle this downsizing process.	5	4	3	2	1	0
I feel physically able to pack, carry, and load all the stuff while downsizing.	5	4	3	2	1	0
The change in my life that prompted me to read this book feels scary.	0	1	2	3	4	5

TOTAL SCORE FOR THIS SECTION: _____

Part 2: The Quantity of My Stuff

	NOT AT ALL				VERY MUCH

	NOT AT ALL					VERY MUCH
I have a lot of stuff that I don't need or use.	0	1	2	3	4	5
I have a lot of other people's stuff stored in my home (like stuff that belongs to my adult children).	0	1	2	3	4	5
I have duplicates of a lot of things.	0	1	2	3	4	5
I have a lot of stuff that I'm going to have trouble picking up and moving.	0	1	2	3	4	5
I regularly declutter the things in my home that I don't need, use, or want.	5	4	3	2	1	0
I've downsized my "material convoy" in the recent past (5 years or less).	5	4	3	2	1	0
I have a lot of unopened gifts and items I've bought that are still in their packaging.	0	1	2	3	4	5
My home feels more full of stuff than the homes of most people I know.	0	1	2	3	4	5

TOTAL SCORE FOR THIS SECTION: _____

Part 3: My Feelings about Stuff

	NOT AT ALL					VERY MUCH
I hold on to too much stuff.	0	1	2	3	4	5
Thinking about getting rid of some of my stuff makes me feel sad, anxious, or guilty.	0	1	2	3	4	5

I am worried that if I let go of my stuff, I'll lose
the wonderful memories attached to it.   0   1   2   3   4   5

I have so much stuff that I don't know where
to start.   0   1   2   3   4   5

I will be less of a person if I let go of my stuff. 0   1   2   3   4   5

I am very strongly attached to my stuff.   0   1   2   3   4   5

The stuff I own defines who I am.   0   1   2   3   4   5

Downsizing makes me think of my
own mortality.   0   1   2   3   4   5

TOTAL SCORE FOR THIS SECTION: _____

Part 4: Legacy Issues

	NOT AT ALL	VERY MUCH

I'm worried that my children or other
heirs will someday fight over my possessions.   0   1   2   3   4   5

I'm worried that my children or other heirs
will someday think my belongings are
not valuable.   0   1   2   3   4   5

I think it's my job to downsize to make
my kids' lives easier later.   5   4   3   2   1   0

I think it's my family's responsibility to
value and hold on to all the things that I
have valued and held on to.   0   1   2   3   4   5

My family members know which heirlooms
are important to my family's history.   5   4   3   2   1   0

I know which items my kids or other heirs
might want to keep as reminders of me
when I'm gone.   5   4   3   2   1   0

I have prepared my will, living will, and all
the other legal documents that express
my wishes if I become incapacitated or die. 5   4   3   2   1   0

My "stuff" is the most important kind of
legacy I can leave to my kids or other heirs. 0   1   2   3   4   5

TOTAL SCORE FOR THIS SECTION: _____

Part 5: Family

	NOT AT ALL				VERY MUCH

My family has a lot of strong and/or
disruptive personalities.   0   1   2   3   4   5

Some of my loved ones are very controlling. 0   1   2   3   4   5

When it comes to resolving conflict,
my family is very emotional.   0   1   2   3   4   5

Downsizing will cause huge fights in
my family.   0   1   2   3   4   5

Someone crucial to the success of this
downsizing (like my spouse or partner) has
a very different vision or goals for this
process than I do.   0   1   2   3   4   5

My family will probably expect me to
do everything.   0   1   2   3   4   5

I think some of my family members will act
in their own interest, at the expense of the
bigger group's happiness.   0   1   2   3   4   5

I think that downsizing will be too emotional
and overwhelming for my family.   0   1   2   3   4   5

TOTAL SCORE FOR THIS SECTION: _____

Scoring Your Quiz

For each section, you can have a possible score of 0 to 40. The lower your score, the more ready you currently are to downsize.

If your score is 0–12, you're already in pretty good shape. But be sure to carefully read the next chapters in order to look for trouble spots you haven't anticipated.

If your score is 13–26, you should allow yourself plenty of time and introspection to get yourself more prepared for the challenge ahead.

If your score is 27–40, you should read this book carefully and really start discussing the upcoming downsizing project with your family and friends, and line up their support.

CHAPTER 2

The Unexpected Joy in Downsizing

Great art isn't just the result of the brushstrokes you see on the canvas or the notes that reach your ear. The same is true of great writing: Far more goes into it than the words you read.

The genius you appreciate also comes from marks the artist didn't make, notes the musician didn't play, and words the author erased from the first draft.

This makes sense when you stop to think about it. It's why one particular carving, more than all the others, catches your eye at an art fair and compels you to bring it home. Its creator envisioned a beautiful figure within the chunk of log, then removed wood from just the right places to reveal it.

But too often, we don't apply this approach to the spaces that surround us. We mistakenly think that all empty space needs to be filled. We don't appreciate that unfilled space can be beautiful and functional, too.

If your home is like most people's, it probably contains half-completed projects that the kids abandoned a year ago, an old coffeemaker that you keep in the kitchen just in case you need it again, a broken printer that holds up the working printer, and gifts gathering dust in cabinets, still in their packages.

Such homes are filled with what I call *un* objects: things that were unwanted and unopened, that go unused, that are unappreciated or simply unnecessary. Our society encourages "more" as the normal default setting, even when it means more useless stuff.

If the surfaces in your home groan under the weight of objects you don't treasure and value, I promise you this: The stuff you own is not only consuming a huge part of your living space, it's also hiding large swaths of a different life that would provide more joy than the version you're now living. A less-stressed, less-overwhelmed version of you waits in there somewhere, too, but you can't see it.

Your mass of belongings—your "material convoy," so to speak—is parked in front of a door that leads to somewhere better. But you can't even find the door, let alone open it.

WHERE'S THE REAL YOU UNDER ALL THAT STUFF?

Always remember: The paper, plastic, electronics, wood, and fabric clogging the typical home has power because it's not just stuff. Every item in your home is there because you have allowed it into your space. Each has a history, an associated memory, and a cost, though you may not recognize them.

Your stuff displays the characteristics about yourself you choose to value. It tells the world, "This is how I imagine myself. This is how I spend my time. This is what I dream about." Your stuff may tell your story more eloquently than your words ever could.

To a major degree, the things you own help create the person you think you are. When you refer to yourself—when you say "I"—much of what you're talking about is connected to your possessions.

NEW PHASES IN YOUR LIFE NEED NEW STRUCTURES TO HELP THEM THRIVE

A second marriage (or third, fourth, or so on) comes with built-in challenges that can threaten its survival, notes psychologist Patricia L. Papernow.

Discussing these challenges in her book, *The Remarriage Blueprint*, author Maggie Scarf writes that "essentially, the remarried family's difficult and completely unforeseen job is to leave behind many of their old assumptions about how a 'real family'—i.e., a traditional, first-marriage family—is supposed to operate and get to work on self-consciously planning, designing, and building an entirely new kind of family structure that will meet their own unique requirements."

The same holds true when you reach any kind of downsizing milestone that puts your life into a new format: retiring, losing your parents, or seeing your grown kids move out of the house (or, for that matter, move back *in*).

You can't assume that the old structures in your life will support this new phase. You have to modify your customary ways of doing things and set up your home to be a physical structure that nurtures and encourages your new life. Ask yourself the following questions:

1. What sorts of new opportunities do I want to enjoy in the next phase of my life?

2. What challenges might keep me from making the most of these opportunities?

3. How can I modify my home, my possessions, my relationships, and my point of view to make the new life I want possible?

The clothes in your closet present the identity you want to display. The world understands your clothes' messages, just like members of the military can read each other's entire careers in the insignia on their uniforms, or hospital employees recognize their coworkers' roles by the color of their scrubs. If these people put on a different uniform or other scrub clothes, they might pass as someone with a different story.

Your books, magazines, and Web pages in your tablet's search history provide a sense of your education, occupation, and political views. Conversely, the ideas contained in their paragraphs work their way into your mind, nudging your imagination and point of view in new directions.

The size and location of your home itself give clues about your income, your age, your tastes, and perhaps your cultural identity. Everything you own in that home—all of it—creates a record of where you are in your life and the path you've taken to get there. It also can predict where you're going, if you let it.

As I've noted already (and will keep reminding you), many of the items throughout your home are also tied to particular feelings. A lot of them evoke happy thoughts. But too often, others bring up a pang of sadness, anxiety, or guilt. These may only feel like a vague discomfort that you don't fully notice. But even then, these feelings can still affect the direction you take, just like a hidden magnet makes a paper clip slide around a table.

The possessions around you can keep you locked into a particular life. But I'm guessing that as you look around your home, you know that you didn't consciously choose all these possessions that represent you. Nor did you keep them in your home for all the right reasons. Maybe they kind of showed up and never left. Maybe it's time for some of them to go.

Not maybe—definitely!

Downsizing presents a unique opportunity to pause long enough to critically examine the objects surrounding you. It's a chance to unburden yourself—before you step into your new life—from the stuff that's keeping you from who you really want to be.

So here's your chance! Now you can consciously choose what stays and what goes. Now you can decide, with clear intention, what's truly important to you. Now's the time to disinvite the things that no longer have a place in the life you're creating.

That goes for your unwanted belongings *and* all the unwanted emotions and memories attached to them.

CLEAR AWAY STUFF THAT DOESN'T REPRESENT WHO YOU ARE

What new turn is your life taking? How are your circumstances changing? Are you getting a new home, a new spouse, new stepkids, or a new career responsibility? Or have you been handed the very unfamiliar challenge of dealing with your parents' home, with or without their presence and cooperation?

Your life is giving you new opportunities. But with all your stuff piled around, you may not be able to see them. You'll have to sort through your layers of stuff in order to find these opportunities and seize them. Letting go of the following things will also free you to become more open, authentic, and true to yourself.

- Objects you never really liked
- Things you regret having paid so much money to buy
- Stuff you inherited and hold on to out of a sense of obligation
- Outdated belongings that identify a version of you that vanished long ago

Think about the possessions in your home. Do they represent the person you want to be right now? Do they present the best version of who you could become? As you go into the next phase of your life, will you be steady on your feet or will your stuff pull you off-balance because it's tugging you back into the past?

If you were to break up and downsize the layer of stuff that announces who you are, what would you look like underneath?

How much of the stuff in your home that represents who you think you are is actually there because of these factors?

Laziness. These are the possessions you don't even care enough about to throw away. "I don't really need this stuff or even want it. But it's not hurting anything. I'll do something with it some other time."

However, we have limited space in our homes to display items that influence our moods, and the mood these items help create is this: meh.

Forgetting to check the calendar. We outgrow possessions all the time: Our clothes get too small or go out of date, our interests change, technology becomes obsolete. So we buy new versions. But the stuff we no longer use stays behind, like hundreds of time capsules hanging in closets and setting on shelves.

Inattention. You buy things on impulse all the time without really thinking about why. Maybe you're bored or hungry, depressed or anxious, or the tag simply has a low enough price. Your attention may flicker for just a moment, but these things linger a long time.

Obligation. These are gifts or inherited items you didn't really want and rarely use. But the idea of tossing them out makes you feel guilty, so they've remained in your home.

Imposition. Have your friends or adult children stored items in your basement or spare rooms, but "forgot" to come back to pick them up? Have you patched up a quilt for a friend or repaired a garden tool for a neighbor, and it's still waiting for the owner to come get it? Does your club expect you to keep supplies and equipment in your home, or does your business partner want you to hang on to old inventory that you'll never use?

You don't need all this stuff. It's concealing who you really are. All you need to keep around are the items that you treasure and the items that you use. That's it. These are things that don't prevent the world from seeing who you really are. Instead, they celebrate what you're all about for everyone to see.

How could you capitalize on this turn that your life is taking in order to create a more accurate identity, one in which a smaller number of possessions—which are more carefully chosen—better represent who you are? How could other, more meaningful aspects of your personality shine through? Instead of stuff, what could you use to fill your time and space?

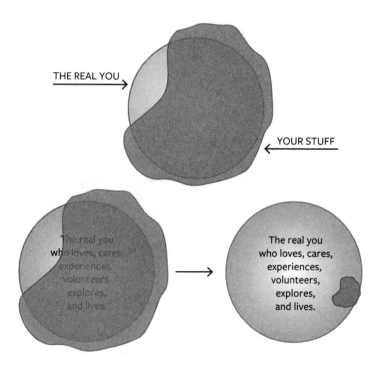

Real-World Downsizing Discovery

Angela says: Get rid of the mental baggage, guilt, or whatever you had from a previous relationship or from your upbringing. Once you do that, your marriage can mature.

In today's society, we often forget that we can put our time, money, and attention to better use than gathering material goods. Once you've reduced your household to a lighter load and set up a new home (or you're no longer caring for your parents and settling their estate), perhaps you can devote more of yourself to:

- Your marriage or other primary relationship
- Friendships
- Kids and grandkids
- Learning, whether from a library or a community college class
- Experiences (in other words, spending money on *doing* rather than *having*)
- Volunteering
- Spiritual exploration, whether your journey is in a church, a book, in nature, or in meditation

It's amazing what happens when you empty a space of physical stuff. With the clutter gone, the vacant area is ready to be filled with an air of peace and calm, a sense of purpose and motivation, and an environment that's welcoming and nurturing.

It's no accident that we talk about feeling "buried" and "suffocated" when we're living in a cluttered space. With the overwhelming piles of stuff gone, you feel more free.

Think of all the open territory that you could create in your life! (It's the lighter portion in the illustration on page 45.) What else could you do with it? On the other hand, what would happen if you headed on to the next portion of your life without clearing this space?

WOULD YOU REALLY WANT AN UN-DOWNSIZED LIFE?

If you continued to hold on to all your stuff, you might be less likely and able to make new memories. Your life might be like an old-fashioned roll of film with all 24 photos already taken—or in more modern terms, your hard drive might be full, with no room left for new home videos, pictures, songs, and maps to new places you want to see.

If you're on the verge of retirement, will the last years of your life find you literally navigating around all the physical stuff you spent your first 65 years gathering? How much attention will you devote to dusting your old mementos and carefully watching your step lest you fall and break a bone?

If you're about to move across the country for a new job, what will you do in your spare time? Create a shrine to your old home, where you can sit and pine away for your old friends and reminisce about how your old job was easier?

If you're getting married for the first time, what will you bring to the home? The toys from your childhood through early adulthood, your neon bar sign, the furniture you bought with an old boyfriend? If you're getting remarried, will you jam the contents of two homes side-by-side into a new house so tightly that there's barely room for the marriage license?

When your final parent passes away, what kind of unity will your original family preserve after you divide up your parents' belongings? Will you and your siblings drift apart now that mom and dad aren't around to pull you together at holidays?

POSSESSIONS MAKE MILLIONS RELUCTANT TO MOVE LATER IN LIFE

Since the early 1990s, an ongoing research project called the Health and Retirement Study has been collecting information from middle-aged and older Americans.

In 2010, the study asked participants about their possessions. Sixty percent said they had more belongings than they needed. (I'd suspect that a much higher number of people truly have more than they "need.")

Another question included in the survey revealed the stress that people feel about downsizing: "Think about the effort that it would take to move your belongings to another home. How reluctant to move does that make you feel?"

Thirty percent said they were "somewhat reluctant." Nearly half—48 percent—said their pile of possessions made them "very reluctant" to move.

"Well, 78 percent of people over the age of 60 say they have

Will fighting over their heirlooms be your last act as a family?

These are the kinds of scenarios that can await downsizers when they:

- Load their boxes in a hurry
- Fail to stop for a moment to think
- Don't look within themselves and at the spots in their relationships that need repair
- Don't let go of the past
- Hold on to things out of a sense of obligation or misplaced family responsibility
- Don't open themselves up to future possibilities

reluctance about moving because of dealing with their things. Multiply that times the number of Americans who are over the age of 60, and you have about 45 million people who have this on their minds," says David J. Ekerdt, PhD, a downsizing-late-in-life expert from the University of Kansas.

So let me ask you the same questions: What thoughts are on your mind about downsizing? How reluctant are you to move possessions to a new home? What's triggering your foot-dragging? Is it the physical challenge of picking up and packing all that stuff? Is it the sense of having your life in upheaval until you're resettled? Is it because change is scary? Or does the idea of parting with some of your familiar possessions feel unsettling?

If you have that sense of reluctance, don't keep carrying it around. Take a closer look at it, figure out where it's coming from, and take steps to address it.

Even fewer downsizers give thought to the impact their stuff will later have on their kids or grandkids. As you get older, what kind of legacy related to your possessions do you want to leave to show that you were alive?

Do you want the generations following after you to share stories about your calm and strength? Do you want the family that you've led for decades to continue the traditions and values you honored? Do you want your kids to pick up family heirlooms and tell their kids the stories related to them (and by extension, related to you)?

Or do you want to leave your family a houseful of meaningless clutter that's dotted with personal treasures? Your kids might wind up throwing out mementos that could comfort them

(continued on page 52)

Downsizer Honors Departed Loved Ones but Leaves Space for Her Own Life

Over a short period of time, Debra Clements brought so many of her family's possessions into her home that her *own* life began disappearing.

Her older sister, who was dying of cancer, would frequently make requests such as "I'd like you to have this. Everytime you wear this top or everytime you use these plates, think about being with me." So Debra kept them. When her sister asked Debra to take boxes of other items to the donation center, she kept those, too.

Ten months after her sister died, her mother took a fall and soon passed away.

Around this time, Debra moved to a new home. "I had all my mother's stuff and my sister's stuff, and I started to put it all on display in my new house, but thought, 'Nothing here is *me*. I'm just rebuilding my moth-

er's lounge room' [living room in Australian]. I also realized, 'What I'm doing is re-creating my childhood, and for someone in her midfifties, that's probably not a good spot to be in.' "

The death of yet another loved one—a close friend named Peter—led Debra to the breakthrough that she didn't need a lot of *stuff* to remember those who'd gone. Though Peter had wanted Debra to keep his collection of hatpins, she wasn't allowed to have them.

"I was really devastated. I held on to that a long time with resentment. Then a friend pointed out how *un*valuable stuff is. She said, 'You don't have that hatpin set. Does that change your relationship with Peter?'

"I said, 'No, it doesn't.' She asked, 'Do you love him any less?' 'No!' 'Then what's the purpose of taking on another possession when it doesn't make a difference to your memories or to the relationship that you had with him?' "

Debra immediately let go of her resentment about the hatpins. Then she let nearly all of her sister's possessions go, too.

"A few years prior to their deaths, my mother, sister, and I went to the UK and Ireland. My sister bought me this beautiful mug, milk jug, and teapot at Bewlies, a famous place in Dublin for tea. One of the things she said to me was 'Every time you have a cup of tea, I'm having one with you.' " Debra had heard that before—but this time, she made the conscious choice to follow her sister's suggestion. She kept the tea set and a string of her sister's pearls. Everything else went to new homes. She also pared her mother's possessions down to a manageable number.

As she created more room in her home, she opened up mental space for new pursuits. Now she's a clinical hypnotherapist who helps clients who are trying to lose weight, cope with disease, and manage anxieties. "None of that would have happened if I hadn't released this stuff. I think to move forward, you need to have a sense of freeness and lightness about you rather than being weighed down by memories," she says.

"The more stuff you have, the more you're weighed down. I think it comes down to that one sentence. The less you have, the lighter you are. Everything you have in your house or your storage unit . . . just because it's out of sight doesn't mean that it's out of your mind."

Real-World Downsizing Discovery

Brenda says: We are not moving to a smaller home, but I am trying to get rid of "stuff." As I have gotten older, I have come to the realization that the stuff clutters my mind as well as my house… and most of it has no meaning to me. I have a disabled child, a teenager in college, and an elderly mother who lives with us, so my life is already complicated enough. Plus, my life experiences have brought clarity to the fact that material things really don't make life better or happier. I am a work in progress, but I'm not giving up on achieving simplicity!

and remind them that they're thankful for you because they didn't understand the meaning of these objects!

Or maybe they'll cling to bakeware you never even used or a book you never even read because they have the incorrect idea that you valued it. They'll carry forward an image of you that's less accurate than it could be.

Also, if you leave your kids and grandkids a giant mess to sort through and fight over, you'll be leaving a family that's weaker and more fractured, and that's bearing a memory of you that's not as positive.

So don't just heave your boxes into the moving truck with the idea that you'll downsize someday after you get settled in your new home. Don't load up a pile of your parents' stuff and haul it across the state—or country—in the hopes of getting to it one day.

Don't stumble into this next phase of your life hoping to figure out what to do when you get there. Let this book help you sort it all out *now*!

I promise you that the extra time and focus you take now to

look at the other side of your possessions—the emotions buried underneath them and the opportunities that lie beyond them— will be a small investment with a powerful payoff when you arrive at your next stop.

In the next section, I'm going to help you dig deeper in another way. When you envision downsizing, what obstacles do you suspect may slow your progress? I'll discuss the most common complications and help you dig into them to uncover tools that create a speedier, more satisfying process.

LET IT GO EXERCISE 2:
The Objects That Identify Me

When strangers encounter me, I hope they think of me as: (insert adjectives that describe you)

_____

_____

_____

What top three possessions that I own help me create that impression?

_____

_____

_____

What possessions that I own would create the opposite impression?

_____

_____

_____

When loved ones and close friends think of me, I hope they think of me as: (insert adjectives that describe you)

_____

_____

_____

Which three possessions help me create that impression?

_____

_____

_____

What possessions that I own would create the opposite impression?

_____

_____

_____

What are the most important roles in my life that identify who I am? (example: parent, supervisor, choir member, scientist, Scout leader)

Which three possessions help me create that impression?

What possessions are linked to roles that aren't important to me, or that used to support roles that are no longer important?

After I'm gone, I would want my children or grandchildren to remember me for these characteristics, things I did, or experiences I had:

Which three possessions will help me leave these memories?

_____

_____

_____

What possessions that I own would create an impression I wouldn't want to leave?

_____

_____

_____

PART TWO

Turn Your Downsizing Stress into Strength

Have you ever realized that downsizing offers a chance to upgrade your outlook and reinforce your relationships? If not, I wouldn't be surprised. After all, when you're going through a downsizing-related transition, you're pretty busy with stuff—and the only end result you've probably pictured is getting this stuff safely to its new home.

That's perfectly understandable. We miss out on all sorts of cool and useful discoveries because we're looking in the wrong place. Gaze at the FedEx logo closely enough and you'll see an arrow pointing forward in the space between the *E* and the *x*. (That's kind of cool!) Examine the fuel gauge on your dashboard and you'll likely see *another* arrow, this one pointing to the side of the car where your gas tank door is located. (If you regularly pull the wrong side of your car up to the gas pump, that's a very useful discovery!)

If all you picture when you think about downsizing is distress and hassle, look again. When you find the right perspective, you'll come to see its hidden benefits.

In this section, let's check out the four main obstacles that keep people from doing the type of downsizing that provides incredible gifts. I'll show you how to reframe these four obstacles so you can use them to your advantage. By the end of this section, you'll be ready to start downsizing your home (or your parents' home) and begin the next phase of your life!

Reframe Your "I'm Losing Something!" Obstacle

I've been describing downsizing-related events as doorways into new, opportunity-rich stages of your life. But traveling the distance from your current life to this new life can feel upsetting. That's especially true if your need to downsize a loved one's home has dropped into your lap unexpectedly.

On a well-known list of stressful life events called the Holmes-Rahe Life Stress Inventory, you'll find the common downsizing milestones near the top. The 10 most stressful include death of a spouse, divorce or separation, death of a close family member (such as a parent), marriage, and retirement.

I'm anticipating that most of the people reading this book are downsizing for one of these reasons. If not, I'm sure one or more of the other stressful life changes on this list apply to you right now: a big variation in your finances, a new home, a new line of work, more arguments with your spouse, a new mortgage, a work promotion, adult kids moving away, or your spouse's retirement.

So as you navigate through this transition, your day-to-day stress level will almost certainly be higher. This is the case even when the downsizing event is going to bring *good* changes, like a higher income with a new job or more visits with family to enjoy during retirement.

That's because downsizing-related events trigger hardships that you can't always control. Maybe your accent is going to sound out of place once you move a thousand miles away. You're worried that it will identify you as a newcomer—but you're even more worried that it will fade away.

Or perhaps you can no longer ignore that a lot of your identity came from being married to a powerful corporate executive or from being the parent to successful student athletes. Now that job is gone, or your last child has pulled out of your driveway for her new home.

Maybe you keep encountering little reminders that you don't have your parents around anymore—like a stranger now using the phone number they had for 40 years. Or your older brother is becoming even more abrasive now that dad isn't around to keep him in line.

When you're already feeling a sense of loss, the thought of

Real-World Downsizing Discovery

Susan says: We have moved seven times in the last five years, each time to a smaller place. We live in a very uncluttered one-bedroom apartment now. Moving was tough, but getting rid of stuff was great! Our family heirlooms are very old photos, and we keep them in a place of pride. The only thing I miss is my fabulous 7-foot couch that was as big as a twin bed (what a great place for a nap!). Everything else was just stuff. Maybe I've missed a kitchen gadget or two, but I can improvise.

Luckily, my husband and I get along great. Otherwise, I don't think downsizing would have worked. The main lesson has been this: Home is where your loved ones are.

shedding your familiar possessions, which help connect you to who you are, can feel even more threatening. Even if you try to be brave about it and say, "It's just stuff," you've put a lot of yourself into your belongings, and they influence how you feel at a level you don't always fully detect.

The idea of losing this stuff can keep you from downsizing thoroughly. But when you understand this feeling, you can use it to your advantage. Instead of *losing* anything from your life, you'll see that you're creating a new home environment that improves your mood and continually reminds you of the best experiences you've enjoyed.

YOU'RE LIVING IN YOUR HOME IN MORE WAYS THAN YOU REALIZE

Wherever Sam Gosling, PhD, goes, a Sherlock Holmes reference usually follows. The professor at the University of Texas at Austin has spent years cultivating a sometimes-eerie skill set that rivals the fictional detective's: how to peer into people's minds by examining clues from their environment.

The way you decorate and fill your home echoes your personality, your desires, and your preferences. These are characteristics that help form your identity. Your home, in turn, has great power to affect your mindset.

"It's a two-way street here. We do things to our spaces that reflect who we are. Then these things reflect back on us and shape our actions," Dr. Gosling says.

You have three main types of connection to the stuff in your home, he says. One is that you scatter what he calls *behavioral residue* around the place. "These are like the kind of clues Sherlock Holmes would look for—it's essentially evidence of your behaviors," Dr. Gosling says.

Do you clip your nails on the couch while watching TV, or

do you go somewhere more discreet? Which upholstered chairs around the dining room table are occupied by adults, and which by children? You and your family leave answers to these sorts of questions that are as telling as your fingerprints and DNA.

This is fascinating info, which Dr. Gosling discusses in his book *Snoop: What Your Stuff Says about You*. But there are two other ways that you're connected to your home that are more important when you're downsizing.

First, your possessions display your identity, as I mentioned in the previous chapter. This is worth repeating, because it's a big cause of the unsettled feeling you may have when you think about downsizing.

"We call these identity claims. There are lots of places you see those kinds of things, not just in people's homes. You see it on bumper stickers or T-shirts or the quote some people put on the bottom of their e-mails," Dr. Gosling says. "There's a lot of research into something called the self-verification theory, which says that people tend to be happier, healthier, and more productive to the degree they can bring others to see them as they see themselves."

So displaying who you are through your possessions is a normal activity, though it's possible to go too far in identifying yourself through your stuff. (I'm certain that I've spent more time convincing someone to part with a shirt than a surgeon might in discussing a major surgery with a patient before the operation.)

Second, we outfit the spaces in our home (and car and office cubicle) with so-called *thought and feeling regulators*. "Lots of objects in our spaces are there to make us feel a certain way. We've done research showing that people try to elicit different ambiances in their spaces. They may go to quite extensive lengths to do that, but they don't always know that's what they're doing," Dr. Gosling says. "They won't be able to tell you that 'I'm trying to evoke a sense of family here, relaxation there, or romance there,' but that essentially is what they're doing."

It's a bit like how you'll choose the music for a particular activity. The playlist you'll select for your workout is very different from the digital music TV channel you pull up during the holidays, which is different from the old-school music you rock out to on your way to your class reunion. Each will put you in a particular mood, which is why you choose it. But you aren't necessarily aware that you're deliberately changing your environment to steer your emotions.

Dr. Gosling and I agree that the objects we place around us affect us on an unconscious level. "Yeah, I think they absolutely do. But we really don't have much self-insight into it," he says. He has a special interest in the photos that people display of themselves. "I'll ask, 'Why do you have that photo?' Often, they give me an uninformative answer: 'I like it.' I know! But why this one? There are 10,000 photos of you that exist in the world; how come this one made it? Often they're not good about knowing why."

So of all the thousands—perhaps millions—of objects that you've touched in your life, why did the objects now in your home stay there? Well, aside from all the reasons we've already discussed (they have a function, they have a memory attached to them, and they help you establish your identity), chances are they also comfort you in some way that you can't exactly put your finger on.

You've radiated your personality into this environment, and it influences your mood. Signals travel back and forth between you and your home, and these signals are transmitted by the objects in each room. The moment you touch your stuff, you get closer to your emotions, especially if you're downsizing. But you may not be fully aware of it.

When you have this sort of relationship with the stuff in your home, of *course* it's difficult to shed your belongings and move on. "Because we're so unconscious about it, we don't always

Real-World Downsizing Discovery

Tahnee says: I always joked I was a bit of a hoarder, as my mum and both grandmas were. It was funny until I was diagnosed with motor neuron disease at only 31 with two small children. I didn't want everyone having to sort through "my precious stuff," so I downsized. I had a happy ceremony going through my personal items from growing up that I knew meant nothing to anyone else and would be thrown out when I was gone. Then I let them go.

While sorting through them, I found lace handkerchiefs my grandma made me for my wedding that were in the bottom of a box with some damage from rats. I was so heartbroken that I hadn't looked after them. So we cleaned them up and treated them with respect in a frame that I hung on a wall in a place of honor. We also made a pile outside of what I chose to throw out when downsizing. Anything that didn't fit went on the pile. The kids were singing the "Let It Go" song as we burned EVERYTHING on that pile! I realized the time I had left was more important than any "stuff." Downsizing by letting it go brought much more of a focus on what really matters.

know what we're going to miss or what we aren't going to miss," Dr. Gosling says.

The first step is to recognize that your work begins before you even select the first item to keep or let go. You've already been doing this work in the activities in Chapters 1 and 2. Acknowledging the many connections between you and your stuff is critical for downsizing in a healthy way. Hopefully, you're already putting a name to some of the feelings you have about particular possessions. (*"Ah, that's why I've never been able to throw this thing away."*) The upcoming process will bring some tough moments, and your stuff will throw you some surprises. Expect that. Anticipate it when you can. Know that such moments are normal.

You'll also have to *reframe* how you look at your stuff. In the literal sense, reframing means taking a picture out of the old rectangle that holds it and putting it into a new one. This new frame, when chosen well, highlights the best aspects of this picture. It improves the image.

In the *Let It Go* way of downsizing, reframing also means shifting the way you view each particular challenge. It may look like an obstacle, but I guarantee that it's also holding a solution for you to find once you look at it in a different way.

Downsizing presents an amazing opportunity to reframe your entire outlook. Afterward, your stuff will play a different role in expressing your personality, and it will have a different effect on your mood.

DOWNSIZING LEADS TO A NEW POINT OF VIEW

Every year, a city's worth of people lose their possessions swiftly and unexpectedly. In 2013, more than 360,000 homes in the United States caught on fire. Nearly half of the homes in the country are located in areas of high risk for tornadoes, wildfires, floods, earthquakes, or hurricanes.

When a disaster takes away their stuff—all those items that comfort and summon memories and express identity—victims often tell the TV or newspaper reporter that they've refocused on what they still have. The tragedy forces them to *reframe* what's valuable to them.

They're grateful for their loved ones and pets, and they realize the value of the kindness that friends, neighbors, and strangers offer at these times. They're sad that they lost their personal treasures, but recognize now that the stuff wasn't really so important after all—certainly not when compared with being alive!

Downsizing allows you to access this healthier point of view without the trauma of losing your possessions to an event outside of your control. My goal with this book is not for you to let go of *all* your stuff, as if a flood just swept away your home. I want you to keep cherished items on your shelves, in your closets, on bookcases, and in china cabinets. I want you to still express yourself through objects and take comfort from them. I want you to keep the stuff that's truly important to you, as long as they are things you treasure or things you use, *and* they fit reasonably and comfortably into the space you have. I'll show you later in the book how to identify these things.

Every day, we decide how we're going to prioritize the elements of our lives, including the things we own, our relationships with family and friends, our time, our view of the world, and our values and beliefs.

Too often, people rely on their stuff to provide comfort. *Way* too often they calm their anxieties and boredom with it. When their paycheck arrives, they buy more of it. They buy a bigger house to store it in. They measure their time on Earth by the height of the pile they've acquired.

Other people throw themselves into relationships in an unhealthy way. Having healthy interactions with others is a key to happiness. But relationships become a problem when you expect them to meet unrealistic needs. Also, not working to understand the other person, or demanding more from the relationship than is reasonable, severely limits your happiness. So does taking too much from the relationship and not giving enough back to replenish it.

Too often people fear their mortality, rather than feeling reassurance about the opportunities they have during their

WOULD YOU RATHER?

In downsizing, the equation isn't "Letting something go = loss." In fact, *keeping* stuff can cause a loss.

Have you ever played "Would You Rather?" It's a silly game in which your friends ask you to choose between two competing (and usually equally unappealing) options. Would you rather eat a week-old pizza or take an ice-cold shower? Would you rather dye your hair pink or shave off one eyebrow?

What if we took this game and applied it to your happiness, your relationships, your possessions, and your home? Where would you place importance and value?

- Would you rather have your mother's wedding dress or a relationship with your siblings?

- Would you rather have your entire set of collectibles that fills one room, or enjoy a smaller home that costs $300 less per month?

- Would you rather have a garage full of stored boxes or room to park your car out of the weather?

Often these are the sorts of options you face while downsizing—but you only realize what your choice involves when you dig deep enough to find it and reframe it. (*"Wow—that fight over the wedding dress did put some distance between us! I wish I'd known those were the two options before I made the decision."*)

remaining lifespan. They don't fill their remaining time with experiences and human connections, because they're dwelling on the portion that's already spent. Obsessing on the past can lead you to hold on to what I call memory clutter. These are items that remind you of an important person, achievement, or event from the past. Worrying too much about the future can cause you to collect "I-might-need-it-someday" clutter. Honoring the past and preparing for the future are both important. But having too much focus on your mortality can hinder you from enjoying the life you have now.

On the other hand, many people give too little time and attention to their life's meaning. Where are their internal compasses pointing? What achievements are worth remembering and celebrating? What kind of mark do they want to leave, and how do they want to be remembered by their families? Often people don't give these questions enough thought.

Now is the perfect time for you to do so. What will mark *your* achievements after you're gone?

And finally, most people leave little focus for themselves. I'm not talking about the vast amount of time that they spend worrying about their health, looking in the mirror, or posting pictures of their dinners online. I'm talking about cultivating a deep understanding of how to live their lives to the fullest. Most people just don't do enough to nurture and feed themselves.

When these elements of your life aren't properly balanced and well-maintained, your stuff entraps you. Relationships cause pain, and your mortality is a source of fear. You're confused about the meaning of why you're here, and, deep down at the core of your being, doubt grows.

So I ask you: What aspects of your life receive your emphasis and time? The priorities you've made before this downsizing will have a marked effect on the next stage—unless you make an effort to change them now.

I'm not in a position to give you all the answers that will fix your life from top to bottom. I don't have those skills, and that would take another book (several, actually), and you don't have time now, do you? You have downsizing to do!

But by realizing that your life may currently be out of balance, committing to changing the imbalance, and then following the downsizing plan in this book, you'll be off to a great start. When you let go of your old ways of looking at your possessions, you're going to begin rearranging your emotional landscape.

Remember, the environment you've created in your home affects your mood, your thoughts, and your identity.

Confronting and changing your thoughts and behaviors can be difficult and time consuming (ask anyone who's spent years in therapy!). By comparison, tossing out certain possessions, reframing how you feel about the ones that remain, and refashioning your home to support a happier frame of mind—in other words, the *Let It Go* process—is straightforward and definitely achievable.

The result is a bit like finding the remote control for your brain between your couch cushions, pointing it at yourself, and pressing the right buttons. You won't necessarily find the enjoyable show you're seeking on the first click, but keep going and you'll get there.

You may find that your top priority becomes your *self*. Notice I didn't say "yourself," meaning you're living with a self-centered focus. What I mean is that you're clear about who you are. You don't need so much stuff to provide comfort and establish your identity. Hand-in-hand with this change, you feel more confident about your *meaning* after sorting through your past and thinking about how you'll use this next phase of your life. You have a better-established sense of direction and better-defined goals now.

This process can also provide a sense of peace about your (or

DOWNSIZE NOW RATHER THAN LATER

Speaking of mortality, if your grown children have been begging you to downsize your household, it may be because they're worried that clutter is presenting a threat to your safety. Plenty of people wait too long to pare down their possessions, and when they're finally ready, they realize that their health problems or physical limitations present a serious obstacle.

Taking care of it while you're physically able is a healthy way to show your stuff who's in charge and acknowledge that you won't be around forever.

your parents') mortality by helping you better understand the memories and values you want to leave to your kids and grandkids or other heirs.

In terms of relationships, if you have a spouse or partner, the *Let It Go* way is intended to be a collaborative approach. The effort you make to inspect your household's possessions—and explore the meaning they have to you individually and as a couple—can create a deeper level of intimacy and appreciation. Depending on who else is involved in the downsizing, such as parents, siblings, or children, you're likely to find an enriched connection in these relationships, too.

And finally, as you move on to your next home, your next job, or whatever the new phase of your life might be, you'll proceed unencumbered with meaningless or unneeded items. You'll have less focus on the *amount* of your stuff and greater happiness with the *quality* of the treasures that surround you. The possessions you carry forward will support your daily activities, bring you joy, resurrect happy memories, say something important about you, and perhaps serve as treasured heirlooms after you're gone.

In this process, you don't lose anything. You gain far more than you knew was possible.

SQUEEZE ALL THE VALUE FROM YOUR POSSESSIONS THAT YOU CAN

Every possession you want to bring with you must *earn its keep*!

For starters, if you have a treasured item that's linked to an important story in your mind, make a record of that memory so you're not the only one carrying it. If you were to suddenly pass away without sharing your story, this possession becomes just another object of questionable value to your spouse or kids.

"Was this thing important to him? Are we supposed to keep it? You take it—I don't want it!" your kids might say. But if they knew that yellowed speeding ticket from 1980 wasn't just a piece of trash, but the reason why you were in the county clerk's office where you first set eyes on their mother, they'd be more likely to tuck it into a scrapbook to commemorate an important moment in their lives.

This point came up during a conversation with Jennifer Lodi-Smith, PhD, an expert on how our identity evolves over the course of our lives. Keep an object "if it connects to a really important moment of your life. If you don't have space for it, take a picture of it and write down the story of this important object; then you'll have a digital legacy," she suggests.

Very soon, you'll be keeping the treasures that are extremely meaningful to you and parting with others that don't make the cut. The following advice is critical: If a possession is important enough to keep, record its story! "Most things we keep are only

PASS ALONG YOUR STORIES TO YOUNG PEOPLE WHO'LL KEEP TELLING THEM

When she lived in Florida, where seniors who've retired and down-sized to smaller homes are an abundant natural resource, Carolyn Curasi, PhD, became interested in the relationship between older adults and their possessions.

"This was something I became aware of because seniors talked about how hard it was to decide what possessions to get rid of and what to bring with them in their move to Florida," she says.

Later in life, memories can present a problem that possessions help solve. You have decade upon decade of stories you want to remember, but your ability to recall them may fade. "I think it becomes even more important in old age, when the memory isn't quite as sharp, to have these devices that remind you and bring you warm memories," says Dr. Curasi, who's now the associate director of the Center for Mature Consumer Studies at Georgia State University.

When it's time to pass certain items to another generation, they become a sort of "inalienable wealth," she says—in other words, a kind of treasure that's permanently associated with the

important with the story. Keeping that information in the family is really key," Dr. Lodi-Smith says. As you get into your later years, you may have more trouble recalling these stories if the importance of the object fades with time. So do it now!

Write them on a notecard so your loved ones will see them in your handwriting. Or make a minute-long digital video or sound recording, or just write 100 words on your computer and send it to the Cloud, where it won't be lost.

Apply this idea to your other keepsakes. If a box of pictures is worth keeping, it's worth the time to identify the people in the giver. She noticed that seniors often put a great deal of thought into determining who would be the best person to receive these treasures.

"They tell stories about why a particular ordinary-looking item is important and about the history of that item. Then seniors often transfer this very valued possession to the younger family member who they feel knows the story the best and who will retell it so the story and the object's meaning will not be lost," she says. "Often they're teaching a love of art, a love of the outdoors, honesty, integrity, and values that are important to the family."

As you're deciding which objects to keep as you downsize, give thought to possessions that will spark your memories later in life and that you can pass—like little flames—to younger people who will keep their stories going. If you're helping your parents downsize, encourage them to share the stories of their treasures and start thinking about who should receive these items.

pictures and perhaps jot a few words about what they were doing. If you're going to want one of your kids to keep a china set, be sure to include a note/video/recording of where the set came from, and perhaps a notable memory from a meal that was served on the dishes.

And if you're ready to let a treasure go, consider taking a picture of it, then adding your story to it. Sometimes just having the picture is enough to preserve an interesting anecdote for your family to remember.

Collecting stories can provide benefits in another direction,

(continued on page 76)

Three Milestones Bring Highs, Lows, and a Need to Pass Down Family Memories

Nancy Little's downsizing story feels like a condensed version of this entire book. Her experience includes the ups and downs of smart estate planning, unexpected family conflict, and big breakthroughs. Now, the 57-year-old needs her family treasures to share her story when she can no longer tell it herself.

Nancy's parents had created a living trust that split their property between Nancy and her two siblings. Also, over time, "We'd said, 'I'd like to have this, I'd like to have that.' The three of us knew about certain things that would go to certain people," Nancy says.

Even so, after their mother died in 2003, the downsizing hit a snag. "My sister got upset about the value of things and thought we should have an appraiser come in and appraise every item down to the saltshakers, so when we split it up, it would be to the penny." A lawyer estimated that this could cost $30,000.

Nancy awoke one morning with a plan. The siblings would declare that nothing in the home had monetary value. They would draw numbers to choose items they wanted, with the understanding that they'd keep anything they took, and not sell it. At the end, they'd sell anything unclaimed and split the money.

The plan worked, but with repercussions. "When you're at the family home, the whole sibling dynamic is right back where it was when you were 12, and all those emotions come roaring out. My sister, who was the middle child, brought up so many things from when we were kids," Nancy says. "We were always close, but after this, there was a barrier."

Sadly, they had little time to reconcile. Her sister developed pancreatic cancer the next year, and Nancy would soon be sorting through her sister's possessions as trustee of her estate.

"So what difference did any of this make? It made no difference," Nancy says.

Now her life has reached another downsizing point. As she was sharing her story, she'd lived 3 years longer with advanced breast cancer than her doctor had predicted.

"When I got this diagnosis, it was a wake-up call. I had 33 bins of Christmas stuff! My kids don't want that, and my husband doesn't either. A friend of mine—who's a pretty organized person—came over, we took everything out, and I got rid of so much. The stuff that's left is the stuff the kids will probably want."

The family treasures that came to Nancy through her parents and sister fill one steamer trunk and a cedar chest. She also keeps a few treasures on display in her home, so she can talk about them with family when they visit.

"Last year, I had another friend come over, and I told her all the stories of everything that was in my trunks. I wanted to write the stories down so my kids and nieces and nephews would know what this stuff was, since they weren't there when my grandma was talking about it," Nancy says.

Those stories will be waiting for these young people when they need them. Nancy knows they'll make their own decisions about her belongings. "My daughter is not a sentimental person. But she did assure me, 'Don't worry, Mom. I'm not just going to go through and throw stuff away. I'll look at what's there, but I'm not taking it all,'" Nancy says. "My mom's doll meant a lot to my mom, but I didn't need to keep it. Even though this stuff means a lot to me, it doesn't mean *they* have to keep it. But they have the opportunity to learn from it."

too. If you're helping your parents downsize before they move into assisted living, they may find consolation in knowing that their stuff will go on to a new life with people who will appreciate it. As a Facebook follower who works with seniors and helps them downsize wrote to me, "As long as I can promise that their things will go to someone who will take care of them and enjoy them, I haven't had any trouble. Just today, I showed a woman a picture of her deceased husband's (now vintage) Florsheim mod ankle boots on a 22-year-old hipster kid I gave them to who was thrilled to have them, and she teared up and was so very glad."

On a related note, if you have multiple items of a similar nature that represent an activity you enjoy—whether they're coins you've collected from international vacations or golf trophies from the local country club—give careful thought to whether you need all of them. One or two of them will be the most meaningful and important, which means that all the others dilute the impact of the best ones. Keep the few that mean the most to you.

When you do tasks like these, you're honestly editing yourself. You're cutting out the stuff you didn't want anyway. You're jettisoning the parts that no longer fit and turning the spotlight on the parts that you want to receive more attention. Meanwhile, you're reallocating the focus you give to different areas of your life so that you'll spend time on the elements that provide the most lasting value.

Now let's move on to another obstacle that derails many a downsizing attempt. As Tolstoy said, "All happy families are alike; each unhappy family is unhappy in its own way."

Poorly planned downsizing has a way of deeply disrupting even a happy family. But when you downsize the right way, you may be shocked by the harmony that a squabbling set of family members can find.

LET IT GO EXERCISE 3:
The Stories of My Life

Go back and review the worksheet you filled out at the end of Chapter 2. Look at the items you noted that most thoroughly describe your identity or the image that you want your heirs to remember. These will likely contribute to the pool of treasures that you take with you.

Choose five treasures from this group that you suspect you'll be keeping. Jot down the story of each of these five treasures in the space below. (Or if you'd rather pull out your smartphone and make a brief video that tells the story, do that! Just make sure you send the video to a storage space that will keep it safe.)

Treasure: _____

Story: _____

_____

_____

_____

Treasure: _____

Story: _____

_____

_____

_____

Treasure: _____

Story: _____

_____

_____

_____

Treasure: _____

Story: _____

_____

_____

_____

Treasure: _____

Story: _____

_____

_____

_____

CHAPTER 4

Reframe Your "I Don't Have Time!" Obstacle

Over the years that I've been helping individuals and families declutter their homes, one of the most common excuses I've heard for why they couldn't get organized is "I don't have enough time."

In these situations, I usually counter with, "You make time for what you think is important." It's true. If something is important to you, you'll always find time for it. If it's not, you'll always find an excuse for avoiding it.

When it comes to downsizing, you may have good reason to feel as if you don't have enough time. But I promise you this: You'll find it. And if you downsize properly, you probably won't need as much of it as you expect.

The reality is that many of the milestones that require downsizing come with built-in deadlines. If you don't get finished packing and moving on time, your missed deadline might be costly.

As I've mentioned, research involving older people found that they typically made their downsizing-related move in just 8 weeks. That's not much time. But you may find yourself in an even bigger rush, like I did.

When it was time to sell our family home, my siblings and I had only 1 week when we were all available to work together. My mother was already in assisted living, and her house had to be decluttered, painted, staged, and put on the market in 10 days. The whole process—even for a professional organizer with a small army of siblings—was daunting.

Depending on your local market, you might find a buyer for your home within a few weeks, or even days, of putting it up for sale. If you're moving between rental homes, you'll likely hurry to move out to minimize paying rent on two places. If mom or dad is moving to long-term care, you may need to empty out their home quickly and sell it to cover their expenses. Or you may have to sort through their possessions under the deadline of an upcoming estate sale.

Of course, a lot of other tasks are filling your plate during this time, too—perhaps you're checking out new schools, obtaining a mortgage, traveling between cities, or scrubbing the baseboards thoroughly enough to please the landlord or the new owner. Maybe you're only able to tend to these chores on the weekend, while you juggle your job and your kids during the week. Maybe you need to take frequent breaks due to your health or fitness limitations. (Downsizing can be physically exhausting.)

If you're asking, "Peter—if you already know how stressful downsizing is, why are you giving me *even more* tasks to do? Why can't I skip all this self-examination and preparation so I can go get these boxes packed?" I'd have to say those are valid questions.

But I don't recommend extra responsibilities for no good reason. I devised the *Let It Go* way of downsizing to achieve two purposes: It reveals the life-improving gifts that many downsizers never discover, and it should actually *save you time*!

The extra time and attention you're already devoting to preparing for the downsizing will speed up the actual process once

TWO DOWNSIZING TIME-SAVERS

As you're downsizing and sorting through items in your home, try to be as logical and methodical as possible.

- **Always sort like things together.** This enables you to see how many of any particular type of item you have (like reading glasses, office supplies, and screwdrivers). You'll be better able to choose the best or the newest to take with you.

- **Leave these things for later.** Photos, scrapbooks, and personal letters or documents usually create the greatest distraction—and they'll be the quickest to delay or derail your downsizing. Box up such personal items and leave them for sorting once everything else is done. I guarantee that the moment you start leafing through these things, you'll find yourself losing time to nostalgia.

you begin. For example, if a loved one has veto power over your downsizing decisions—like a spouse or sibling—you'd better believe that this person has the ability to slow down the timetable or even bring movement to a halt. I'm going to help you create a proactive plan for teamwork ahead of time, which will prepare the path for speedier downsizing.

Another reason why the *Let It Go* method moves more quickly is because it streamlines the decision making that could otherwise swallow epic stretches of your precious time. And believe me, this easily happens!

"Do I need to keep this hand-carved tiki statue I bought in Hawaii? That was such a good time! Except for the huge fight we got into the day I bought this statue! My life is so much better now that I'm divorced. But I sure wish I had more money so I could travel like I did back then. Should I go through with

this retirement decision, or should I keep working for a few more years?"

Downsizing often triggers these stream-of-consciousness diversions that waste hours. The strategies I'm going to show you will help you sort through your possessions quickly so you don't get sidetracked by stress, nostalgia, or worries about the future.

I'd like to teach you the most important *Let It Go* time-saving strategy now. By the end of this chapter, you'll be prepared to speedily handle your central downsizing activity.

YOUR BIGGEST TIME-SAVER: KNOWING YOUR THREE TYPES OF STUFF

All the stuff you own will fit into one of three categories: Memory Items, I-Might-Need-It Items, and Trash/Recycling. It's easy to determine where each goes, and this will be your first task when you start doing the hands-on downsizing work.

Once you categorize each item, you can quickly determine whether you'll keep it or let it go.

Memory Items

These are the things that remind you of important people, achievements, or events from your past. You have four kinds of Memory Items, and you'll only keep the first kind: the treasures.

The treasures represent the peak experiences of your life and the most important moments from your family's history. Their worth is not measured in money, but rather in the meaning and significance they hold for you or your family. You would continue to feel the absence of your treasures for a long time if you lost them.

A treasure is truly irreplaceable. You can't buy another in the store, and you probably wouldn't even find this thing on eBay if you searched every day for a year. In my own case, a treasure would be my mother's green dessert plate (which is insignificant and of no value to anyone else, but a real gem to me).

Even though you can quickly and easily picture many of your treasures, beware: Treasures can really slow your downsizing. That's because people tend to have Treasure Creep. Even though they don't really meet the true definition of treasures, many items still seem valuable enough to keep. Because you're so afraid of losing a treasure, you'll draw a wide perimeter around them and wind up including stuff that doesn't really meet the criteria.

The fear of losing a treasure may also add to your nagging sense of dread about downsizing. But *any fear you feel is going to slow down the process*, and you don't have time to waste. Remember: Treasures are few, important, and deeply meaningful. Once you identify your treasures and know they'll be safely coming along with you, you'll be able to apply your full attention to managing the next task.

In my experience, treasures represent about 5 percent of the objects you own, or even less. I definitely want you to keep these items, so long as you absolutely, positively verify that they are indeed the most important and special things you own. In Chapters 7 and 8, I'll give you a handy way to determine whether you're keeping too many treasures. For now, spend some time thinking about the items that you'd truly give this label (that would be the best, the most significant, and the most memory-laden items that you own).

Once you make your selection, I want you to have the confidence to let these go from your mind. Since you're sure you won't be leaving behind what's most important, there's no reason that any worry about this group of items should be bogging down your decision-making processes.

You also have three other kinds of Memory Items. These you

don't take with you. These go somewhere else, whether you give them to friends, sell them in a garage sale, or have a cleansing ritual where you burn them in a bonfire.

- **The trinkets.** These are items that you've collected from family holidays or celebrations that spark a smile but aren't as important as the treasures. Examples: the Grand Canyon shot glass from your Arizona vacation or the broken pocketknife that grandpa owned that no one remembers him carrying. With you downsizing to a smaller home and beginning a new and exciting phase of your life, now is the time to let trinkets go.

Real-World Downsizing Discovery

Janina says: In a recent 2-week period, we sold our 2,500-square-foot home and our 1,800-square-foot cabin. We had a lot of belongings to sort, pack, move, and store, and then begin the house-hunting process once again. It's very difficult to know what to give away when you don't know where you'll be living yet. So my advice to anyone is to only keep things that are practical and that you love.

Most important, if you feel "irritated" by a certain artwork, piece of furniture, or anything else in your home, it is not worth holding on to it simply because someone close to you gave it to you or you inherited it from your parents. Your home is your castle—not theirs!

Little did we know that we would end up buying a home that equaled the square footage of our two previous homes put together! But we are so thankful we got rid of most everything that was not useful in our lives or that we had outgrown emotionally before we moved in.

- **The forgotten.** These are the items that usually make you laugh and shrug your shoulders when someone asks where they came from. "I have no idea!" you'd say. If an item has no significance other than it's been in your home longer than you can remember, then today's the day to let it go, too. Examples: the paperback that a random person who had a crush on you gave you in high school, or leaves you pressed in wax paper on a random rainy Saturday in your youth.

- **The malignant.** These are items that remind you of negative or painful moments. You hold on to them even though their very presence in your home triggers a memory or emotion that you'd prefer not to have. It's time to let these go now. Take a moment to honor the younger version of yourself who survived this event, revisit any take-home lesson the object teaches you, and get rid of it now. Examples: the bike helmet you were wearing during the serious wreck, the journal you kept during a painful breakup, or the travel brochures for a vacation you had to cancel years ago so you could attend a funeral.

It's possible that a friend or family member might want some of your trinkets and forgotten stuff. Or, these items might be valuable enough to sell. Whether it's through gifting, donating, or selling, let these items go. And for the malignant items? You're beginning a new day that has no place for anything that evokes a painful memory. Let them go . . . into the trash!

I-Might-Need-It Items

These items have a useful function. The I-Might-Need-It category contains books and magazines on your shelves, clothes in your closet, food in your pantry, office supplies in your desk, and maybe even stuff in your kitchen junk drawer.

I'd estimate that about 80 percent of the stuff in a typical home falls into this category. But you're not taking all of it!

You're only going to bring one kind of I-Might-Need-It Items with you. I call these the *worthy* items. These are things that will reasonably and comfortably fit into the new space you have, which you use regularly *and* will likely continue to use after your move. A blender, for example, is a worthy item. Your winter coat is worthy, too.

But if you have a blender and a chopper and three other kitchen devices that turn food into tiny pieces, you probably don't need them all. If you have three winter coats, you probably don't need all of them—and if you're moving to Key West, you may not need any.

Your worthy items must have a readily visible purpose in the next stage of your life, and you need adequate space to store them appropriately. You must have a better reason for keeping them than "I just don't feel like getting rid of this yet" or "I can't make a decision now, so I'll box it up, take it with me, and deal with it later." No doubt, dealing with worthy items is one of the most challenging parts of downsizing, but the effort is definitely worth the return.

Do you have a current ongoing need for this item (in other words, do you use it often)? Then it's worthy. Do you have a specific plan to enjoy gadgets after your move that you don't currently use? (For example, you've already checked out a golf course so you can swing your now-dusty clubs in retirement, or you've signed up for cooking classes so you can use your kitchen gear.) Then they're worthy.

Are you at least 95 percent sure that you'll want to offer an item to your kids (and they'll want it) in the *very* near future? Then it's worthy, too.

But thinking you might use an item in a year or two or that

PACE YOURSELF, AND SET THE RIGHT TARGET

Two of the biggest factors that lead to fatigue when you're downsizing are doing too much at once and aiming for perfection. To avoid exhausting yourself, especially if your energy or fitness levels are limited, commit to spending just 2 hours a day sorting through your belongings. (If you're comfortable devoting more time, go right ahead!)

Don't try to do everything perfectly. Attempting to do so will leave you overwhelmed, frustrated, and exhausted. Aim for good enough. That's an adequate goal that motivates you to get the job done.

your kids will use it when they graduate from college in 3 years are not valid reasons to call an item worthy.

Now, keep in mind that you also need to establish that you'll have room for these things at your next stop. I'll show you how to do that in Chapters 7 and 8.

It's quite likely that you'll have several options for distributing I-Might-Need-It Items that you don't want to take with you. That's because these items might well be valuable or useful to someone else.

Maybe these are hand-me-down family items that you or your kids no longer need, but you'd like to offer to your nieces, nephews, and other extended family.

Or maybe a nonfamily member would want to buy your clothes, furniture, and other items you're letting go. Should you sell this stuff online? Do you have time to arrange a garage sale? Do you have enough stuff for an estate sale? Or do you donate it to charity for a tax write-off? In the next section, I'll walk you through these strategies.

(continued on page 90)

Late-in-Life Moves Gave Couple More Reasons to Downsize

Donna and Bruce Vickroy, ages 69 and 75 respectively, *think* they're in their final home—or as Donna puts it, their "feet-first-out house." But after three moves in recent years, they're keeping their possessions pared down to a manageable level. Just in case.

They made their first move after Bruce took an early retirement offer. After a "huge estate sale" to downsize their stuff, they left the San Francisco area for a smaller home east in the Sierra Nevada mountains.

Then their son got married and, a few years later, started a family. He wished the Vickroys could be closer so they could enjoy more grandparenting time. So Donna and Bruce found a rental back in the Bay Area and spent part of their time there. But after another grandchild arrived, they decided to sell their mountain home—and the country-appropriate furnishings they'd bought for it—and move back to the city permanently.

The first move "was harder for my husband than me. For the most part, it didn't bother me to get rid of half the kitchen, half the linens, and most of the books," she says. The downsizings have been "considerably easier" for them in subsequent moves—in part because they're thinking more about the kind of legacy they want to leave.

After Donna and Bruce sorted through the belongings that their late parents left behind, which involved some heavy digging, the experience "made us so aware that you really should never do that to your children." Now, when they want to unload an item from their home, they'll offer it to their kids (*without* guilting them into taking it, Donna says).

"If there's something you can use now, take it and love on it," she tells them. "If not, we just don't want to save it any longer. We don't want you to have to deal with it later." Her son, who is something of a minimalist, often passes on the offers, she says. But "my son-in-law tells my daughter every time they leave, 'You've been shopping at Mom-mart,' " she laughs.

At this stage in their lives, the couple is putting a higher priority on enjoying *people* rather than *things*. "In living so close to family and grandkids, we've just placed our values elsewhere. So the stuff doesn't really matter that much anymore," Donna says.

For holiday gifts, they may offer experiences that the family can share, like dinner and tickets to a performance. "This is far more meaningful," she says. "And no one has to dust it."

In their retirement, the Vickroys have fewer possessions to clean and organize. They don't have the sense that they're paying property taxes to maintain a home for extra stuff they don't need. Well, not a *lot* of extra stuff, anyway.

"Yes, there are things that I hang on to," Donna says. "I have a Longaberger basket collection that I'd love to sell, but the market is horrible right now. I'll either wait, or [my family] will have to use them for kindling!"

Trash/Recycling

The things that neither you nor anyone else needs to keep will represent, I suspect, about 15 percent of the stuff in your home.

This is the bag containing a handful of moldy grass seed from 2 years ago, the lone sock, the storage container without a lid, the stack of coffee-stained newspapers or magazines, and the pile of cleaning rags in the laundry cupboard. Trash is the clutter that accumulates—and perhaps even reproduces—under the sink, in the backs of closets, and in the other dark and overlooked crevices in your home.

If it clearly looks like trash, it goes in the trash/recycling pile as you're downsizing. If you keep saying "no" when you try to put it into another category, it also goes in this pile. ("Is this a Memory or an I-Might-Need-It Item? Does anyone else want it? Can I sell it?") Malignant items go in here, too.

So that's the quick-and-easy process of determining what you'll take and how to distribute the rest. Not so hard, is it?

Now, let's discuss how to pull out the treasures from your Memory Items pile and ensure that you're bringing the proper amount.

X MARKS YOUR TREASURES

The treasures in your home are like trophies that the world has given you over the years. However, these aren't the kind of trophies that kids get just for showing up. These are, to continue the metaphor, the trophies you'd get for winning a state championship. These are your very own Olympic medals.

Your treasures commemorate the most loving, memorable, and triumphant moments in your life. They most strongly capture the essence of the most important people who are now gone (like grandparents, special great-aunts, a departed spouse) and those who have moved away (like grown kids or best friends).

Here's a good rule of thumb: If something makes you smile, fills you with joy, brings back a great memory, and makes your heart sing when you look at it, then chances are high it's a treasure. If not, it likely isn't.

Treasures aren't all your favorite items from all your family vacations. They're the *best* items from the *best* vacations—the ones that most vividly bring back the most meaningful memories of traveling with your loved ones. Treasures aren't a shelf of papers you wrote and books you read during grad school—they're the *most important* paper and the *most important* book.

When you have multiple copies of a similar thing—all your child's spelling tests, all your grandmother's quilts, all your stuffed animals from your own childhood—then *one* of them is going to be the most meaningful to you. Maybe it's the highest quality, or it was most important to the person who created it, or you simply have a vividly pleasant memory from the day you received it tucked away in your brain.

But if you continue to keep all the others that *aren't* so special, you lessen the value of the best one. It's hard to locate among the crowd of runners-up. If this thing is so special, why diminish it? Why not elevate it to the place it deserves?

Our natural tendency is often to see *everything* in a home as important, whether we're downsizing our own home or dealing with the items that belonged to a parent or someone else we loved. But I can tell you that when everything is important, nothing is important.

Bringing too much, or filling your home with the items collected during another person's life, will weigh you down and fill you with sadness. Having *more* treasures will not bring a person back, nor will it help you relive an earlier stage of your life. You'll simply feel suffocated and mournful—and that is not how treasures should make you feel.

Each treasure should commemorate a specific memory, event, or person. As you decide whether or not an item deserves to go onto the treasure pile, ask yourself: *"Is this memory, event, or person truly deserving of being honored with one of my limited allotment of treasures? If so, is this the best item I can use to honor this memory, event, or person?"*

However, don't start this process with the object. Don't look around at the items in your home and figure out how you can turn them into treasures by attaching memories, events, and people to them. Instead, take the opposite approach: Come up with a list of the "bests, greatests, and mosts" in your life, then find the treasures that serve as reminders of them.

In the *Let It Go* exercise that follows, I'll provide some sample memories, events, and people to get you started. For each of these entries that you think are important enough to commemorate, go find a treasure. Then come up with your own meaningful entries and find treasures for those, too.

So how many of these treasures can you reasonably take with you? This is something that I've struggled to quantify. Here's the solution I've settled on as an easy way to select a number that should fit in your next home.

Clear off your dining room table. This is now your staging area. However many treasures you can fit on that tabletop is roughly how many you should take with you. This may seem extreme, or even harsh, but it's a measure I've found to work.

I suspect that your dining room table is proportionate to the size of your current home. If you live in a mansion, you probably have a banquet-worthy table that will hold a lot of treasures. (But if your next home will be substantially smaller, cover only a portion of the table. You're picking the treasures that will comfortably fit in your *downsized* home, not this one.) If you're currently in a one-bedroom apartment with a small eat-in kitchen, your little table will still probably be an adequate space to hold the treasures you're selecting.

How high you stack your treasure table is up to you, but this is not a competition to game the system to see how many items you can squeeze into a limited space. If you break the table, that's a sign you chose too many!

LET IT GO EXERCISE 4:
Making My Treasure Map

My happiest memory of child 1:

My happiest memory of child 2:

My happiest memory of child 3:

My happiest memory of grandchild 1:

My happiest memory of grandchild 2:

My happiest memory of grandchild 3:

My favorite family vacation:

My greatest career achievement:

The gift that gave me the most pleasure:

The moment when I felt closest to my spouse:

My most enjoyable family event:

The most important memory I have about each departed relative:

My greatest academic achievement:

The best time I had with friends:

My most important athletic achievement:

My biggest personal triumph:
_____

_____

My "Weekend in Vegas" trip:
_____

_____

My most meaningful childhood memory:
_____

_____

The greatest dinner party ever:
_____

_____

The best birthday celebration:
_____

_____

The happiest day of my life:
_____

_____

The most challenging adversity I overcame:
_____

_____

The time I laughed the hardest:
_____

_____

My wedding day:
_____

_____

My favorite high-school memory:

_____

My favorite college memory:

_____

My most important family heirloom:

_____

The book that had the biggest effect on my life:

_____

My favorite pet:

_____

My most meaningful experience in nature:

_____

What other "bests, greatests, and mosts" in your life will continue to inspire and comfort you after you downsize? As long as they fit on your table, your job is to come up with whatever treasures best represent the life you've lived! (Keep in mind that multiple descriptions can apply to the same treasure.)

LET IT GO BASIC FLOWCHART

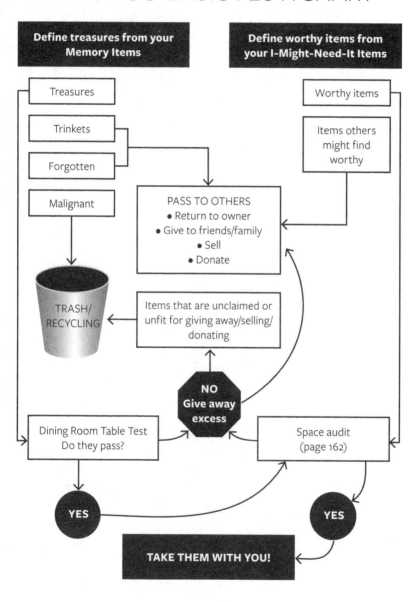

CHAPTER 5

Reframe Your Family Dynamics Obstacle

Nearly every family has at least one "heirloom drama" story after downsizing. Mine is no different.

My father was a decorated World War II veteran, and after he passed away, my sister had strong feelings about where his set of military medals should go: to her. After all, she'd been his main caregiver in the final years of his life.

My older brother felt that tradition dictated who the rightful inheritor of these medals should be: him. After all, he was the oldest son, and these sorts of heirlooms automatically go to the oldest son, right?

One priceless treasure, and two people had compelling stories that they felt were the most convincing reason for keeping it. Sound familiar?

We had peaceably divided up the rest of our father's belongings that our mother didn't want to keep for herself. But these medals derailed the process for my brother and sister, and we all got dragged into the discussion.

My father was a strong, stoic man who was a product of his generation. These medals represented some of his characteristics that my brother and sister wanted to keep close now that he was gone. My siblings were also fueled by powerful, deeply buried values that had resurfaced and collided at this moment.

If a fear of family conflict makes you dread the idea of downsizing, I understand your concern. I've been there. However, these sorts of disagreements and the strong feelings that fuel them are to be expected in times like these.

Downsizing is about so much more than "the stuff." Those medals were essentially just bits of metal and cloth. But to the people who wanted them, they meant something entirely different. Every object carries stories, memories, and emotions. These may be entirely different for each member of your family. An item that you can't even recall *seeing* before might be a deeply significant treasure for a sibling or other family member.

The risk of family conflict and tension is naturally unsettling, but this isn't a good reason for you to dread downsizing your parents' belongings or working with your spouse and kids to downsize your own. Challenging family dynamics are actually a reason to *welcome* the process.

When you understand why people hold particular objects dear, you come to know them on a deeper level: You learn their important memories, their life priorities, and how they view themselves. If an item is significant enough to them that they'll fight over it, explore those feelings! They'll lead you to helpful discoveries about these loved ones.

FAMILIES FIND UNEXPECTED GIFTS WHEN THEY DOWNSIZE TOGETHER

Thus far, I've been talking about how emotions and impulses related to your possessions can steer your behaviors. You may have trouble simply describing these emotions, let alone controlling them. But as you've seen, they're inside you, and they're real.

Now throw other people into the mix: parents, siblings, your spouse, your in-laws, and perhaps your adult children. They bring their own history and their own individual points of view, needs, and conflicting emotions. They have considerable decision-making power over how this process is going to work—likely as much or even more than you. They bring their own agenda and follow their own values.

Maybe you have a terrific relationship with your loved ones, and you can't stand the thought of putting even a little distance between you. On the other hand, maybe you've been arguing with some of them for decades, and you'd have trouble sharing a turkey dinner, let alone difficult family decisions. Whatever the relationship, you have a long history with these people that's going to affect the downsizing process.

Or you may be struggling with a parent who can't cope with the idea of letting go of a household of memories. Or a parent who's insisting that you take home a bunch of stuff *you don't want*! Or a parent who's disappearing into dementia or losing function to a chronic physical illness, and you're anxious about the new responsibility you've been handed.

When it's your *own* home that you're downsizing (this chapter applies to that scenario, too!), perhaps you and your spouse are already enduring a lot of stress leading up to your move. The

Real-World Downsizing Discovery

Jane says: After the cluttered life of raising five children and living in a house, then a trailer, then an apartment, I have learned to let go of a lot. My favorite moment of downsizing was when my daughter said to her boyfriend, "See? This is how our place should look."

idea of just packing everything into the truck to avoid another argument will probably seem appealing to at least one of you. This is a strategy that many couples use. But if one of you wants to downsize and the other doesn't, then this is a conflict that will need to be addressed and resolved.

The thought of downsizing with all of these factors in play may feel like mixing unlabeled bottles of powerful chemicals together. What's the reaction going to be like? Can you and your loved ones control it? Will you come away unscathed or burned?

As difficult as it may be to see them, these fears are concealing more gifts. Take your apprehensions apart and see what's behind them. Yes, emotions can rise during a downsizing, and so can voices. You may have to rehash old issues that you thought your family had left in the past. But by deliberately working through the task, you can transform your connections with the other people involved.

This requires you to be open to the values that are propelling your loved ones' actions and words. Listening to their opinions in an unemotional way may not change the situation, but it will definitely give you insight into how to respond to it.

Find out *why* they seem to want to empty mom's house as fast as possible or *why* they are dragging their feet about making a 2-hour drive to come help you. Don't just be annoyed. Dig deeper. What does dealing with mom's items mean to them? What memory or pain or fear does it touch in their minds?

Find out *why* your spouse can't seem to part with that giant mountain of souvenirs from her childhood. What does it all mean to her?

Now's your chance to learn things about your loved ones that you never knew. As your family dynamics may be shaking up and resettling into a new configuration, now is the time to establish who you will be as you move forward. Here's your opportunity to start this new, shared phase in your lives with success.

DOWNSIZING CAN LEAVE LASTING DAMAGE WHEN DONE POORLY

Make no mistake: When you go about downsizing the wrong way, you can cause permanent injury to your relationships. I see that all the time. Without proper communication and transparency, the process can leave your loved ones deeply shaken. I've heard stories from downsizing survivors who sound battle scarred, even years later:

> My brothers and their wives were throwing out things that THEY thought had no value. Luckily, my husband was positioned near the trailer and managed to save a few special mementos that I remembered from my childhood. Once they are gone, you cannot get them back again, and it just adds to the loss that you are already feeling. Oh, and my brothers did not think about donating the items either—everything was destined for the tip [dump, to an Australian]. These situations can cause deep divisions within families. I know I was angry and hurt by their antics at the time.

And:

> I didn't get anything from my grandfather's house except a picture I had colored when I was in second grade . . . then I found out my cousin had given boxes of my late grandmother's and grandfather's stuff to my sister-in-law (who could not care less). I admit I really had

my feelings hurt that I was not even asked about any of it. I am 43, and my grandmother died of cancer when I was in the eighth grade, and the years we had leading up to that were very special to me. I need to get over it . . . but it really upset me.

Many of the belongings that stuff our homes (and our parents' homes) can easily be cast to the wind without anyone caring about the loss. On the other hand, if you or a family member loses one precious item in the downsizing process, it can leave a sting that lingers for decades:

My 99-year-old grandmother passed away in Hong Kong, and my father traveled to assist his family in clearing out her home. A lot was discarded, and a lot was distributed to local extended family, because it was too big or too cumbersome to be shipped to the United States. My father is not a sentimental man and he's not into keepsakes or mementos. But as someone who is now very interested in family history, I grieve over what was discarded and what is now unobtainable.

And:

My sister, without telling anyone, went through all of my mother's belongings that were accumulated over 50 years. She kept what she wanted and then she and my father had an auction with the rest. If the rest of us wanted anything, we had to go and bid against the public. My sister had the good sense to not show up. That was 26 years ago. The hurt runs deep. Now, if I see something in a secondhand shop that looked like something my mother had, I purchase it and pretend it was hers.

These stories, which fall into worst-case-scenario territory, illustrate how a downsizing event can get out of control. It doesn't matter if someone is being deliberately hurtful or is simply acting thoughtlessly; the end result may be the same. You or a family member could lose items you really wanted. Even worse, the process could drive a wedge into a good relationship.

But this kind of outcome is avoidable. I've also heard plenty of stories of families setting aside their differences to work together, of families tapping into their strengths to weather difficult challenges, and of families employing creativity to prevent conflict and solve the inevitable standoffs before they explode.

My siblings and I found a solution for the dilemma that Dad's service medals presented. It wasn't perfect, but it was good enough. By the way, that's a result that should leave you happy: good enough. You can do an awful lot of fighting and waste an awful lot of time while you look for the perfect solution.

My sister, for the sake of keeping the peace, agreed to my brother keeping the medals. But first, we asked an accredited dealer to create replicas of them, and the rest of the siblings received an identical set. Did Dad ever wear *these* medals on his uniform 70-plus years ago? No. But just like the originals, the replicas pay respect to his duty, his bravery, and his patriotism—and they help us honor the man whenever we look at them.

Soon I'll walk you step-by-step through bringing your family together and working smoothly during two types of downsizing: your own (Chapter 7) and your parents' (Chapter 8).

But for now, I'd like to prepare you for some of the personalities, situations, and colliding values that you might encounter when you and your loved ones dive into a group downsizing project.

(continued on page 108)

GENDER TRADITIONS HOLD MANY FAMILIES IN A DOWNSIZING RUT

When parents recruit their families for a downsizing project, the participants often divide into two teams: men on one side and women on the other. Typically, they then distribute specific types of family treasures within their own team.

That's what downsizing expert David J. Ekerdt, director of the University of Kansas Gerontology Center and the main researcher for The Household Moves Project, and a fellow researcher found when they surveyed 36 households. In each family, parents over the age of 60 had recently downsized in order to move into a smaller home.

"Couples, when asked how they worked both together and independently, often explained that the husband packed *his* areas of the house—generally the garage, basement, and other workshop-type spaces—while the wife would pack *her* areas—usually the rest of the dwelling.... While the distribution of work was unlikely to be equal—the garage versus the main house—couples rarely addressed the fairness of this arrangement," the researchers wrote.

In several cases, couples acknowledged that the wife did *all* the sorting work. One husband, given the task of sorting a box of his family's letters, only got as far as reading them. Another refused to downsize "his" stuff and carted it all directly to the new house. Another 70-year-old widower simply told his daughter and his late wife's friend to decorate his new home. "I said, 'You gals set it up; I'll live in it,' " he reported.

Daughters were more likely to help downsize than sons, especially with sorting through possessions. They also tended to provide leadership for the process. (Daughters-in-law more often worked to set up the *new* home rather than sorting through family treasures.)

Sons tended to drive moving trucks and handle tasks like picking and managing estate sellers.

Downsized Objects Often Travel by Gender

Items that an elder man in the family used, or that were regarded as "men's stuff," were usually passed on to sons, grandsons, nephews, and sons-in-law: tools, guns and other hunting gear, military uniforms, bow ties, and hobby equipment.

The matriarchs typically passed down "their" objects—china, jewelry, seasonal decorations—to the women in the family. Often, they also tapped younger women in the family to become the next caretaker of family photos and memorabilia. In several cases, adult daughters' homes became warehouses for items that they expected their own daughters to take in the future when they had their own households.

Gender-based shortcuts can save time, and they may work for your family. But they also present a well-worn rut that can lead your family away from the *best* solutions. These traditions can also lead to resentment if they overrule a family member's desire to play a certain role or take home a particular item.

During your downsizing process, avoid assuming that women will wrap the china and men will load the truck. In your family's case, maybe the best recipient for camouflage clothes is a sister, and the best caretaker of a decorative glass bowl will be a 12-year-old grandson.

Also, please don't allow yourself to be guilted into accepting an heirloom you don't want. And *don't* allow your own home to become a warehouse for family objects that you'll redistribute someday when your kids are older. Someday may never come, and you'll be stuck with a home that looks more like a memorial to someone else's life than a reflection of your own.

You don't have to follow society's traditions—set your own rules!

THE SEVEN PEOPLE YOU'LL
MEET WHILE DOWNSIZING

As nice as it would be if everyone could sit at the table and make downsizing decisions based on logic and unbiased discussion, that sort of process doesn't always happen.

Instead, a quiet sibling who always felt overlooked seizes this opportunity to finally have his voice heard. Another who was mom's special confidant expects you to heed what she *really* wanted but never told anyone else. Maybe dad's way of mourning is to just leave behind the memories and move on.

It's important to acknowledge that everyone involved in a downsizing event is being influenced by his or her own values. Don't be surprised if family members bring ancient arguments or slights to the table or resurrect memories that others forgot long ago. In many cases, they may have trouble identifying these values or feel embarrassed or vulnerable about discussing them. But it's possible that the values motivating them may be right out in the open.

Also, be ready for your fellow downsizers to seem a little different. Their values, along with their personality quirks, may cause them to play a role that you weren't expecting. Keep your calm if a familiar loved one suddenly becomes one of the following characters during downsizing. In fact, don't be shocked if someone actually plays *more* than one of these roles at different times.

1. The Control Freak
2. The Denier
3. The Procrastinator
4. The Businessperson
5. The Provocateur
6. The Peacemaker
7. The Attention Seeker

Real-World Downsizing Discovery

Linda says: I could not let any items go that held memories of my mother. I finally realized that I had to live for myself and create a home that was all mine! I finally came to the best solution for letting go of so much that she held dear.

Since she did so much to help animals, I have donated a tremendous amount to Animal Aid of Tulsa in her memory. She owned a large collection of collectible plates, and whenever my church has a fundraising auction, I donate a few plates, making certain they are auctioned off in my mother's memory. With books that she loved, I place a sticker on the inside cover noting that I donated them in her memory. Whoever gets the book sees that and knows that my mother was loved.

Also, I gave pieces of furniture that my mother purchased decades ago to my closest friends. Although they are now out of my home, I feel as if they are still in the family since my friends have them. This was the only way that I was able to start letting go. My mother's memory now goes on in so many others' homes and lives!

When you witness a loved one acting like one of these characters, keep in mind these three rules.

1. Resist the urge to engage. Avoid responding to the role that your loved one is playing. No matter how she's acting, this person is still your child, spouse, sibling, or parent. My goal is to help you reach the other side of the downsizing process with an even better relationship, and this may require you to help your loved ones even when they aren't acting their best. The immediate reaction will be to strike back. Don't! Instead, stop. Breathe. Think before you respond.

2. All have a reason for their opinions. Avoid belittling a loved one's needs or dismissing his requests as unreasonable. Dig deeper to understand the value that's fueling his actions. It's never about the stuff. You'll always find an underlying reason for a behavior, request, or demand. A little gentle questioning often reveals the real motive behind what seems like an unreasonable stance.

3. Your way is not necessarily the best way! Each of us is the hero of our own story, and we all want our voices heard. That's true for you *and* your teammates. Ignoring your loved ones' opinions is telling them that their contributions aren't valuable. You would hate to hear that, so don't accidentally say it to someone else.

Plus, a loved one may have good reason to perceive *you* as one of the following disruptive characters! Be sure to understand their qualities well enough that you'll recognize if you begin to play one of these roles!

The Control Freak

Fear makes people do strange things. When faced with a fear-inducing situation, some people instinctively try to exert as much power as they can over it. A sense of control—even if it's only imagined—is calming. However, people who need to have a hand in every decision or exert their will over every situation can come off as the Control Freak.

Every family downsizing requires calm, level-headed leaders. The process also needs participants to handle tasks that are well suited to their abilities. Every team member needs a voice in the downsizing. The Control Freak, however, tries to do too *many* jobs and make *too many* decisions. Their way is the best way— so get in line or face the consequences!

This person may try to exclude other participants, rush the process so others won't notice what's happening, or assume that she's acting in everyone's best interest without finding out if that's true. This approach leaves others feeling disrespected and disempowered. It also creates resentment that can be difficult to heal. The true stories that I included a few pages ago each had a family member who showed characteristics of the Control Freak, and they all left devastation in their wake.

Dealing with the Control Freak is difficult because of his certainty that everything will only work out if you follow his directions. The best approach if you find yourself in this situation is to agree early and often on very clear goals, roles, and responsibilities. Always document who is handling which task, and regularly check back in as a group to ensure that tasks are completed.

When the Control Freak attempts to railroad the group or overstep his or her responsibility, go back to the list of tasks and duties that has everyone's buy in. Calmly thank him for his opinion but reiterate that someone has that area covered. You may have to repeat this a number of times, and you may also have to deal with some high emotion.

Sample scripts you might use include:

- *"That's an interesting idea, John, but we've agreed that Ellen is taking care of that."*

- *"Just a moment, Sue. Before you offer your input on how to do that task, let's ask Eric to fill us in on what he's done about it."*

- *"Please, Mary, we all need to feel like we're contributing equally. Let's let everyone have the chance to pitch in and help make this downsizing a success."*

The Denier

Often people do not go gently into the next phase of their lives. It's also common for their loved ones to refuse to accept that big changes are happening, like illness, disability, or the end of a life.

This happened in my own family when my siblings and I disagreed on whether the time had come for our mother to live in a residential setting. She had become frail but retained her fierce independence. At a family meeting, I recommended that she move into assisted living. I sensed that some siblings agreed but didn't want to rock the boat. She stayed in her house, but only for another 6 months. An upsetting fall in her dark home, alone at 3:00 a.m., made it clear that she needed assistance. But at that point, she needed it in a hurry.

Denial has a way of turning an orderly downsizing process into a situation that's urgent, rushed, and confusing. This is because the denial pushes decisions further down the road. Later, your circumstances—which can become catastrophic—may require a quick decision.

A parent who was lucid and in control just a few months ago may leave you responsible for making big decisions with little information. What kind of long-term care does dad need? Who has power of attorney? Where are the bank accounts? What's the combination on the safe?

You can find the Denier in all kinds of downsizing situations.

- Soon-to-be retirees who don't want to change their lifestyles to accommodate a drop in income

- Young adults who are engaged to be married but don't seem to realize that living as a couple involves compromises

- Grown kids who aren't interested in making their own decisions and are happy to continue letting mom and dad do so

- Anyone who's about to move into a smaller home but refuses to whittle his or her possessions down to an amount that will fit into the new space

Remember, the Denier has reasons to interpret reality differently than you do. Odds are good that they're not in denial just to frustrate you—they are struggling with the situation at hand,

TIME CAN BRING MORE CHANGES LATE IN LIFE

Time has a way of behaving strangely when you're dealing with older parents. Six months may not seem very long when you're 30 or 40 or even 50. But for people in their eighties who might be a little frail, 6 months is enough time to go from good health to complete dependence on others. So if a loved one is denying that an older parent or other relative is declining, be sure that someone is carefully monitoring this person's health changes.

and this is a powerful tool to keep reality at bay. Maybe they're frightened of change. On the other hand, maybe they're optimistic and just don't see what you're so worried about. Maybe they see this as God's plan, and it's not up to the family to sort it out. Maybe they're just not emotionally or physically equipped to deal with this challenging task.

Responding appropriately when the Denier is a stubborn-but-frail parent is particularly challenging. Respecting your parents' demand for independence can mean jeopardizing their safety and wellness. We begrudgingly honored our mother's wish to stay on her own, even though we knew that the outcome might be disastrous. (Frankly, it almost was.) You have to find a delicate balance, and there's no one hard-and-fast solution.

When dealing with Deniers, it's important to move carefully, since they are often not coping with what they're confronting. Outline a very specific plan that suggests the consequences that could occur if you don't take action, and what your options will be if these consequences occur. Unfortunately, you may have to accept that your family might face a catastrophic incident before a parent who's the Denier approves of taking action.

Be gentle but firm with your Denier. Understand that the

person you're dealing with is fragile and struggling, but be persistent in discussing the very real situation that he's not allowing himself to see.

Sample scripts you might use include:

- *"This is the situation we're facing."* Include specific examples such as: *"Mom can no longer walk to the mailbox to get the mail"* or *"Dad isn't eating the meals left for him and has dropped 8 pounds in the last month. I think we need to take the following steps."*

- *"We don't seem to know how much risk Dad faces if he keeps living on his own. Why don't we meet with his doctor and get a professional opinion?"*

- *"We only have 1 month to deal with everything that's in the house. Very soon, we won't have enough time before we move. How do you think we should proceed so we don't get into crisis mode?"*

The Procrastinator

This type of downsizing partner is likely to have a similar effect on the process as the Denier. The Procrastinator can't sign forms on time, sort through the boxes you've set aside, or make the *one tiny decision* that will allow the downsizing to move forward. Procrastinators often agree to handle tasks or make decisions but later plead that they hit a roadblock or were too busy to complete them (or they come up with some other grown-up version of "the dog ate my homework").

As a result, procrastination slows you down, adds to your frustration, creates more costs, and may burn up the valuable time that separates an orderly process from a crisis.

But again, the Procrastinator is probably not trying to derail the downsizing deliberately. Just like the Denier, the Procrastinator may simply not be able to make a decision, because then she'll have to accept the reality of the situation she's facing. This person may be scared by the thought of actually retiring after planning for it for years, feel overwhelmed by the need to declutter and sell the family house, or be paralyzed by the idea of living in a much smaller home.

Procrastinators may feel that *not* acting is the only thing they can do to control their world. Or maybe they're unprepared or uninformed, and they don't know how to make the first move. They may feel like you or a sibling is wielding too much authority in this process, and they're vetoing your decisions until their voices are heard. Perhaps the Procrastinator in your life is also a perfectionist, and he's going to take all the time he needs to make the perfect decision, even though these situations seldom, if ever, allow for "perfect" decisions.

Dealing with the Procrastinator is similar to working with the Denier: You need a firm hand and a clear explanation of the consequences that will arise if everyone doesn't finish tasks by deadline. You should also do a lot of documentation. If the Procrastinator agrees to find an appraiser to assess the value of antiques in your home, then put that commitment in writing and come to an agreement on the deadline for the task. Also agree that if the Procrastinator doesn't handle tasks by a particular time, then you (or another family member) will step in and handle them as you see fit. This approach respects the role of this family member but also acknowledges that time is important and commitments must be honored.

Sample scripts you might use include:

- *"Everyone, let's make a list of which tasks need to be completed in the next month and who'll do them. We also need a deadline for these to be completed, and names of who will step in if they're not finished on time."*

(continued on page 118)

Doctor Urges Older Patients to Downsize at the Optimal Time

Karen Cadman, MD, a physician living in Southern California, has seen the benefits of scaled-down living in her own family, and she regularly prescribes a dose of downsizing to her patients.

"My average patient age is somewhere between 70 and 80. My office is near many nursing homes, assisted living facilities, and several large, independent senior living communities, and the issue of downsizing and moving comes up almost daily," she says.

During her medical training and early career, she moved frequently—and easily. In her midthirties, she asked herself, "What happened to the days when I could put all my possessions in a van? I wanted a house that I wouldn't have to spend so much time cleaning." So several years ago, she and her husband sold their 2,200-square-foot house and downsized to a smaller home.

Recently, her parents and in-laws both downsized, encountering different challenges in the process. "For my parents, in their midseventies, it was more a lifestyle choice to age in an independent-to-assisted-living environment that would provide for their care as they got older. I don't think they realized how much work it required to maintain their previous home until they moved," she says.

For her in-laws, who are in their late eighties, "part of their motivation for downsizing was to prevent their kids from having to deal with all of their stuff," she says. (That is one of the best gifts aging parents can give their kids, by the way!)

Since then, "they have had a harder time integrating and leaving their old life behind, even though they are only 2 miles from their previous home and have many friends and acquaintances already living in their new community. Surprisingly, they had a much easier time downsizing their material possessions; it was harder to give up the perceived change in independence," Dr. Cadman says.

When her parents downsized their considerable collection of stuff, Dr. Cadman had to be creative in protecting the space in her own home. "My mother felt better giving things away to people she knew rather than selling, donating, or trashing on her own. My brother and I agreed to take anything they offered us, no exceptions, just to help them reduce. Because I live closer, I was the recipient of a lot of their larger items," she says.

She sent some stuff to her brother, but quietly donated or threw out a lot of other items. She also converted treasures into keepsakes that were easier to store or use. She had a bunch of her baby clothes converted into a quilt. Damaged pieces of her grandmother's china

became earrings and pendants for her female relatives.

"As difficult as it was for my parents and in-laws to downsize and move, I was really proud that they made the decisions on their own when they did. I have watched many seniors not do it well! Sometimes a crisis precipitates a move—like dementia, a life-changing injury, or an accident like totaling a car—which is the worst-case scenario," she says.

"It's a disaster watching family members try to hurriedly find a more suitable living arrangement while simultaneously downsizing without the help of their parents," Dr. Cadman says.

"When I advise seniors about moving to a smaller home or an assisted living environment, I usually tell them to move *before* they think it's time, while they are still healthy enough to participate in the process."

- *"Tom—can you please give a date and time when this will be completed that works for you?"*

- *"Leanne, which of these tasks can you finish by the end of day Thursday? If I don't hear from you by then, I'm happy to follow through with them."*

The Businessperson

Let's be clear: When you're downsizing a home, it's imperative to look at this process as a family business. Like any business endeavor, the downsizing-related milestone requires you to handle money in a responsible and transparent way. You'll have laws to follow and legally binding forms to sign.

You should hold meetings that follow agreed-upon rules. Someone should keep clear notes about actions that participants will take and responsibilities that they agree to handle. To-do lists with deadlines should go to everyone. This is serious business and should be handled as such.

"Officers and stakeholders" in your downsizing business will have differing degrees of voting power—maybe a lot (your spouse when downsizing your own home or your parents with full cognitive ability who are downsizing theirs), maybe a little (a parent who's completely incapacitated due to stroke or dementia and didn't leave any wishes in writing), and maybe somewhere in between, based on the mood of the group (like spouses, cousins, or grown children).

But sometimes a different sort of Businessperson with a capital *B* arises. This is:

- The unofficial accountant who halts the process by making sure all distributions are equal to the penny

- The brother with inside knowledge on the local real estate market who is trying to get dibs on rental property that will gain more value

- The sister who wants formal rules that allow no wiggle room
- The hard-nosed tycoon, the sneaky wheeler-dealer, the inside trader, or the hostile-takeover planner in your midst

These are the more extreme cases. Chances are, the Businessperson who arrives at your downsizing is a family member who simply sees his business acumen and experience as invaluable to the project. This person may often seem to be more about the *process* than *empathy*. In the face of high emotions, his hard-nosed business sense can seem insensitive and rub others the wrong way.

Even if you'd like her to be a little less CEO and a little more kid sister, when dealing with the Businessperson, your best strategy is to acknowledge her expertise and use the business tools of project management, agendas, to-do lists, accountability, and task assignments to steer her energy.

Sample scripts to consider include:

- *"Amy, if I speak with the family and put together a list of everyone's main concerns, could you draw up an agenda for our first meeting and perhaps chair it so we stay on task?"*
- *"John, we have a lot of tasks to get done in a short period of time. Could you possibly get everyone on board with a timeline, then project-manage for the next couple of weeks?"*
- *"Erica, can you suggest the best way to track the expenses each of us will have when downsizing the house so we can be sure everyone is reimbursed when we're done?"*

The Provocateur

Remember when grandma let you have that silk scarf when you were 12, but you shouldn't have gotten it because you were grounded? No? Your cousin certainly does, and all these years later, she's ready to even the score. Many families harbor a

Provocateur like this who will emerge during tense times such as downsizing.

This person will try to disrupt the delicate decision-making process that the other participants have agreed upon, stir up dissent, and use this opportunity to settle injustices that no one else recalls.

It may be abundantly clear when you're dealing with a Provocateur. Sometimes they operate openly in their daily lives, and they've brought drama to a long line of family decisions (you know, the person who stirs up trouble every holiday and isn't happy at a special occasion until someone's crying). But you might be surprised when an unexpected Provocateur pops out of the closet.

The Provocateur could be an out-of-state aunt or uncle who announces a claim to a family possession, a brother- or sister-in-law pulling strings behind the scenes while working through one of your siblings, or even a parent who's playing family members against each other by giving valuables to a favored child.

Keep in mind that grief or fear could be fueling a Provocateur. Someone who is grieving or scared may lash out as a way to cope. Refrain from giving the Provocateur what he wants, which is a big reaction that provides a diversion from the issue that's important in the moment.

As difficult as it may be, the best way to deal with the Provocateur is to ignore the sting in his comment and address the issue rather than the hurtful delivery style. When you rise to the bait, you're rewarding his unwanted behavior. Further, engaging the Provocateur or getting into an argument simply distracts everyone from the task at hand and delays the downsizing process. Instead, try to defuse the Provocateur's anger.

Sample scripts you might use include:

- *"Okay, Tony, if you want to talk about that, we can, but it will have to wait until we've dealt with our scheduled business."*

Real-World Downsizing Discovery

Tauna says: A few years ago, my mom and I were looking through holiday photos, and she noticed how cluttered everything looked with her normal things out in addition to her holiday decorations. She proceeded to try to thin some things out but was having a difficult time with it. I came over and helped her to remember to ask herself if each thing had any meaning and if it made her happy in any way.

Also, I often look through local Facebook pages and Craigslist ads for people in need of things, most often from great loss such as fires or separations from abusive relationships, and let my mom know about them so she can decide if she would like to donate anything. We especially enjoy doing this, because we know it will greatly improve someone's quality of living and really could mean the world to someone. She has told me that she often feels like a small weight has been lifted from her shoulders after going through and getting rid of things.

- *"Angela, I understand you're upset about what's happened in the past, but at the moment, we're focusing on what we have to get done this week."*
- *"I can see that this issue is very important to you, and I'd like to talk about it with you later when we can give it the attention it deserves."*

The Peacemaker

At first sight, the Peacemaker seems like a valuable ally during a family downsizing scenario. After all, you want participants who can anticipate and prevent dissent, soothe hurt feelings, and broker compromises. Who doesn't like peaceable people in a stressful situation?

Be careful what you wish for. Peace that's artificial and forced can interfere with your downsizing! The Peacemaker demands niceness at all times. He insists on always creating a perfectly fair agreement that leaves everyone equally unhappy. He censors siblings' comments, in case they might hurt someone's feelings. He keeps the process synthetically sunny and saccharin sweet.

But this is a family business you're running at the moment, and sometimes business partners need to be direct—or even blunt—with each other. Sometimes the group must make hard decisions in which consensus may not be possible.

A pushy Peacemaker may keep the family from making a tough decision that feels sad in the moment but fits well in the overall picture and is best for all concerned. A Peacemaker's shushing may make a sibling resent feeling unheard. Or the Peacemaker may prevent your family from having the messy, cathartic, and real experience it needs in order to have closure.

Dealing with the Peacemaker can make you look like the bad guy if you don't do it with care. (After all, the Peacemaker seems thoughtful and pleasant. How dare you shut him down?) So accept what he has to say, but ensure that it's not the last word in the conversation. Invite others to express their opinions if the Peacemaker attempts to stifle discussion.

Scripts you might try include:

- *"That's an interesting point of view, Patrick, but let's hear what everyone else thinks as well."*
- *"Anne, not everyone will get their way on every disagreement. That's okay. Let's just make sure that everyone's satisfied and treated fairly in the grand scheme of this downsizing."*

- *"Thomas, let's keep in mind that we have an emotional task ahead of us. It's actually good that people feel comfortable enough to express what they really think."*

The Attention Seeker

A cousin of sorts to the Provocateur, this character always finds a way to turn the discussion back to himself at the expense of continuing the downsizing process.

Perhaps a lonely sister enjoys having a captive audience while the family is gathered to work on this task. Maybe a spouse who deals with stress by using sarcasm and humor won't stop making unfunny jokes. Sometimes it's simply ego, and sometimes it's a self-indulgent need to tell the family, "Hey, I'm here. Look at me!"

Attention Seekers might not be as disruptive to the downsizing process as some of these other characters, but they do distract you from the important work at hand.

As with the Provocateur, the best way to deal with the Attention Seeker is not to reward unwanted behavior. Attention seeking may stem from immaturity, so respond to these people in the same way you might handle a disruptive child. Halt their interruption, insist that they stop their troublesome behavior, and create the expectation that they'll redirect their attention to the task at hand.

Scripts you might use include:

- *"Paul, we're currently dealing with how to dispose of Dad's book collection. If you want to talk about your last trip to Vegas, let's do that over a drink when we're done."*
- *"Thomas, that's not appropriate now. Please stop!"*
- *"Mary, our time is really precious here; we don't have the time to focus on [your issue] right now."*

KEEP LOOKING FOR THE HIDDEN
GIFTS OF DOWNSIZING

The same elements you encounter during a family downsizing project that may stir up trouble—the togetherness, the memories, the personalities on full display—can also leave you in a better place after the process is finished.

Even if they're wearing the costume of an Attention Seeker or Procrastinator, underneath are real people who may feel just as sad, anxious, or guilt-ridden as you do. Their fear and confusion take many forms—just like yours do! Try to look beyond the emotion of the moment to the struggle that your sibling, spouse, child, or parent is enduring.

In many ways, we're all 8-year-old children making sense of the world. This is especially noticeable when we're required to alter the world we've known. Work under the assumption that those close to you mostly want the same things: peace, harmony, and solutions that build rather than tear down family relationships.

Find the people beneath the difficult exteriors and connect with them. This is a chance to get to know who your grown siblings are *now*, rather than forever viewing them as the unfinished people they were in your childhood and teen years.

Also, apply the wisdom you've since gained with maturity. Avoid reverting to your 8-year-old selves who speak without thinking and act without considering the consequences.

I have heard scary stories like the ones I included earlier in the chapter, and you've probably heard friends tell stories like them. In offering those, I don't want to suggest that they're the typical downsizing experience.

I have also heard stories of downsizing that helped heal families and bring them together, like the Missouri woman who told me how she and her sister—separated in age by 13 years—"became best friends during the 2 difficult-yet-glorious months" they spent cleaning out their mother's house after she moved into assisted living.

Downsizing also gives you the chance to better understand who your parents are and what values steer their lives. You can learn what they're scared about or what's giving them strength. Which of these qualities might you want to adopt? Which do you want to keep out of your own life? These lessons don't come along every day.

This all applies even when the family that's downsizing is just you and your spouse. Now's the time to renew your partnership and relearn how to work through challenging, emotionally messy tasks under a ticking deadline. Why not use the tools in this book to repair and reframe your relationship before you bring it into a fresh new home?

Now is the time to reconnect with who *you* want to be, too. Do you have emotions that are causing you to be bossy, disruptive, or angry during this downsizing? By addressing these emotions, you could create space for a healthier point of view.

Which brings us to the next chapter. Many of the fears that lead downsizers to make poor decisions grow from the same three poisonous emotions: sadness, anxiety, and guilt. You may *think* that a certain problem is blocking you from your task, but if you take the time to inspect it closely, you'll likely find one of these emotions lurking behind it.

When you learn how to reframe these concerns, you'll be able to move more rapidly—and happily—through the downsizing process.

LET IT GO EXERCISE 5:
Charting My Family Dynamics

Who else will be participating in your downsizing? If you haven't already discussed how your family members and other participants feel about this event, now is a good time to do so.

Get a sense of whether they're feeling excited, apprehensive, or a little of each. What do they hope to take from the downsizing, either in terms of emotional closure or physical possessions? How do you think they'll support the process? How do you think they might obstruct the process? If you sense they may introduce chaos into the downsizing, or have needs that you'll need to meet, how might you respond constructively?

Jot down a few notes here to help you prepare.

Downsizing teammate 1:

Downsizing teammate 2:

Downsizing teammate 3:

Downsizing teammate 4:

Downsizing teammate 5:

Downsizing teammate 6:

CHAPTER 6

Reframe Your "This Is Emotionally Painful" Obstacle

Sometimes your body feels pain in mysterious ways.

A pain in your shoulder doesn't necessarily mean the shoulder itself is injured. Maybe, because of the way your nervous system is wired, that shoulder pain is actually due to a problem in your gallbladder, located all the way down in your abdomen.

Doctors call this referred pain. Our bodies, it would seem, aren't necessarily laid out like a well-organized home.

If you ignore a discomfort in your arm because you think, "Eh, it doesn't hurt that bad. Anyway, it's just my arm," you could be missing a referred pain that warns of a heart attack.

A similar issue can occur when a downsizing event on the horizon grows closer. You think you're uncomfortable for a specific reason—like the pressure of working under deadline or the physical challenge of moving—but you overlook the actual source, which may be fear of your mortality or the uneasiness that comes with dealing with any emotional issue with your family members.

Each piece of the stuff that fills our homes has a history and a memory attached to it. We might forget where we bought an object or how much it cost, but its ability to trigger an emotion, remind us of a person, or take us back to an earlier moment remains almost constant.

Often these reminders and memories are happy ones. That's a big reason why we buy or keep things—to feel good about who we are and where we've been. A central goal of the *Let It Go* way of downsizing is to give the treasures that summon your positive emotions a prominent place in your new home (or bring these feel-good possessions back from your parents' home).

But to get there, you may first have to travel through a place that's a little darker. You may have to put your hands on items that remind you of times when you were in pain or distress. You may find yourself revisiting an earlier loss.

Plus, parting with items that once brought you comfort and helped define you can be a little scary. Though you're obviously an adult, this is akin to how a kid might feel when giving up a security blanket.

Though you might describe such feelings as "fear," you'll generally find that they're like a referred pain that you can trace back to one of three emotions: sadness, anxiety, or guilt. I call these the SAG emotions for short.

DIG DOWN TO THE TRUE CAUSE
OF YOUR DOWNSIZING FEAR

The SAG emotions often masquerade as specific fears that people feel about downsizing. I'll describe these shortly. But first, it's worth further exploring why downsizing can evoke such strong feelings of sadness, anxiety, or guilt.

Sadness. Downsizing may remind you of elements of your life that are now gone. At these times, you're moving forward, but important people may not be coming with you because they've died, they've moved on to their own homes, or your relationship with them has ended.

Odds are good that some of the hopes and dreams you once had are gone, too. Maybe you already achieved them, and the glory of your accomplishment has faded. Maybe you never fulfilled them, or you wound up pursuing different goals instead. Seeing your high-school letter jacket, encountering reminders from a first marriage, or gazing upon your welding equipment (so much for those plans of being a sculptor . . .) can bring up waves of eye-watering sadness, especially now that you're at a turning point.

Downsizing-related events also simply remind you that you're getting older. You may lose track of how long you've been in your home while you're living in it, but you'll definitely remember when it's time to pack your things. In our society, growing older is not treated as a cause for celebration, and the downsizing process may leave you in quite an unfestive mood.

"Did my whole life amount to this? How did I wind up here? If I'm no longer in the stage of my life when I was at the peak of my game, with the greatest potential, then where does that leave me now?" you might ask.

There's no getting around it: Dealing with reality can definitely hurt.

Anxiety. If sadness is related to the place you're leaving, anxiety is tied to the place you're going. If you're downsizing because you've run into tough times, you may be anxious about when and how you'll start moving in a better direction. But even happy events can be tinged with some degree of anxiety, whether you're getting married or retiring to the relaxing retreat you've been dreaming about for 20 years.

You might be asking yourself, "Am I making the right decision? Is this move going to be good for my family? Who can I turn to for support in this new setting?" Just as we tend to hold on to possessions because of sadness about the past, we also cling to belongings because they might shield us from future distress.

The idea of shedding these things may make you more anxious. How do you know if you'll actually need an item where you're going if you've never been there? Such anxieties can make you question whether you're still a rational person.

"I know the weather experts say it has never, ever snowed in Key West, but the weather's unpredictable these days! What if I actually do need my snowblower after I move down there? I might have a heart attack if I have to shovel the driveway! Why did I ever agree to this move?" Just because your thoughts aren't rational or logical doesn't mean that you're not having them!

Anxiety about fitting in, having enough room, making the right decisions, or upsetting your family are all natural. You're launching into the unknown. So don't be surprised if you're anxious and a little on edge.

Guilt. At some point, everything that's currently in your home was once useful or valuable to someone. Maybe it was important to you, your kids, or your grandparents. And here you are thinking about turning your back on some of it (or a lot of it) and walking away!

The notion of parting with certain items will likely make you feel powerful guilt. I predict that you'll feel this pang at least once while downsizing, especially if you're caught up in the idea that it's your responsibility to maintain the family history or protect the heirlooms. You might get the sense that someone is closely watching over your shoulder, waiting to voice an opinion if you get rid of the wrong thing, whether it's the ghost of your mother or the memory of your sweet little 7-year-old . . . who's now 6 feet tall and bearded. (Again, downsizing can *really* cause you to think irrationally!)

Will your choice feel like you're betraying someone's trust?

Will someone you care about be disappointed, if only in your mind? Will you be dishonoring a memory or disrespecting someone who's passed?

Your loyalty can also be to an object, rather than a person. You've cared for this possession for years—sort of like it was a pet—and now you're telling it that it doesn't rate among your treasures. What if the next owner doesn't take care of this Disney figurine like you did? Will the Snow White in your hand someday be buried in a landfill?

This kind of obsessiveness can appear unexpectedly. You may find yourself deliberating over items that you previously never thought important or particularly valuable. Again, don't be surprised. Dealing with the power of your possessions can be deeply unsettling.

Sadness, anxiety, and guilt can dramatically slow your downsizing process. They fuel disagreements and all-out fights between spouses. They cause you to dwell on the worst possible outcomes that could result from the transition you're making.

The SAG emotions can also cause you to bring way too much stuff into your new home. That's a problem. Even worse, you may not recognize these emotions while you downsize, which means you don't bring them into the light to resolve them. If not acknowledged and addressed, they then subtly poison the new phase of your life.

In the next section, your actual downsizing process begins. But before you get started, I'd like to introduce you to the nine common "fears" that slow down or derail downsizing projects. I use quote marks because these aren't really fears—they're a form of referred pain that actually comes from sadness, anxiety, or guilt.

Once you dig into each fear and find the specific emotion

Real-World Downsizing Discovery

Mary says: When my parents moved in with us, I gave Mom free rein to decorate for the holidays, since I worked 40-plus hours, as did my husband. She and my three boys loved it. After Mom passed away, it was difficult for me to see all those decorations.

Once I got through the first year, I decided to start scaling back, since I had SO much. I only kept a few pieces for some holidays (as for Christmas, well, that is ongoing, but I have thinned it a bit). I've learned a lot from you, Peter, like how you can never throw away a memory. Also, if you have to keep items, don't just shove them in a box and say "someday." Display or give them to someone who will cherish them. Honor their memory.

that's producing it, you'll find that it loses its power. This "reframing" becomes another strength that will help see you through your move. You'll also let go of negative emotions related to your stuff, so the treasures that make you feel good have more prominence in your new life.

#1: I'm going to make the wrong decision.

This is one of the most common "fears" among downsizers. Some items are irreplaceable. If you part with your T-shirt from the rally for the presidential candidate who visited your town in 1992, you're not likely to come across another one again.

On the same note, if you offer a family heirloom to one child, and another child wanted it badly, you can never take that offer back as if it never happened. Sometimes downsizing is a bit of a gamble, and once you place your bet, you're committed to accepting the outcome.

But these feelings aren't a fear. They're an anxiety. We tend to be anxious about situations that feel out of our control. When you let an item go, you lose control over it. If it goes away and you want it back, you might not be able to regain it. If loved ones get upset over a decision, ultimately it's up to them to make peace with it. You can't control their responses.

So reframe that anxiety. Think about it this way: You're gaining more control over your downsizing situation right now! You're picking up the knowledge and tools to make informed decisions that you'll be pleased with in the long run.

Before, you might have had less insight into memories—and the treasures attached to those memories—that were important to you. You may have been unaware of which elements of your identity were central to how you see yourself, and which possessions supported those parts of your identity.

But you know these things now! And before you finish this book, you'll learn more ways to make decisions that will leave you feeling confident and in control. By understanding yourself, your loved ones, and the choices you're about to make, you greatly lower the chance of making decisions you'll later regret.

On a side note, choosing to downsize mindlessly and without self-awareness is a decision in itself: You would be deciding to shirk your responsibility by taking your hands off the wheel. So you might as well make a decision that protects your interests!

Reframing tip: It's very likely you *are* going to make a few mistakes and have a couple of missteps, but that's the nature of working through the accumulation of a lifetime. Accept these as expected moments that don't require anxiety.

#2: I'm going to lose my memories.

It's not uncommon for people to collect ticket stubs from movies they see and concerts they attend. These are a terrific way to jog your memory. Given that they bear the date and location of the show, you'll likely remember the car you drove and who was with you, and you may even remember the outfit you wore and the restaurant where you ate beforehand.

If you were to throw the tickets away (which I wouldn't necessarily recommend you do unless they dredge up hurtful memories, since they take up little space), you would very likely lose these details.

That's a big reason why people are afraid to let things go: They worry that with the objects gone, the memories attached to them will also disappear. That's a valid concern. We tend to get fuzzy about specific events over time, and as we grow older, it's reasonable to want reminders of where we've been.

But this fear is a form of sadness, and it's a sadness that you don't need to carry forward when you're downsizing. I'd like for you to reframe this fear and think differently about it. Realize

KEEP THESE FACTORS IN MIND WHEN DECIDING ABOUT COLLECTIONS

If you have a collection of similar Memory Items—like movie tickets—the two factors to consider when you're deciding whether to keep them are *space* and *significance*.

You'll need space in order to house the collection in a way that honors and respects it. Keeping hundreds of vintage postcards in a box in the garage is not honoring them. When a collection is not treated with the respect it deserves, it becomes little more than clutter.

Second, what's the significance of having *all* the items? Retaining the full collection can be a meaningful memento in some cases. But often, retaining just a few key pieces achieves the same result.

that downsizing gives you the chance to *relive* your memories, perhaps *uncovering* some you've forgotten, and then *preserve* the most important ones.

As you downsize, find some time to explore your photo albums and inspect your memorabilia. Scan through your old journals and cassette tapes. Savor the opportunity to walk through the halls of your own personal museum. Be excited! Be glad that you were alive to make these memories in the first place, that you had the foresight to record them, and that you get to keep the treasures buried in this stuff!

Some memories, however, are too bad to keep. If you encounter objects that give you a stab of hurt instead of a zing of joy, don't hesitate to let them go. Now is the time. Out go the memories of the bad relationship, the college attempt that didn't work out, the hateful relative, and any outcomes that remind you of failure, evoke sadness, or are simply best left behind. You are creating your future, and you have an opportunity here to decide what you'll bring into that future.

Does downsizing still look like a cause to lose memories? To me, it's a chance to *strengthen* the memories that deserve keeping and delete the ones that distract from the good stuff.

Reframing tip: If you are certain that a possession will continue to bring up feelings of sadness in the future, leave it behind. Sadness should never be a factor that motivates you to keep an item. Why should sadness pull you away from the uplifting feelings that your true treasures will evoke?

#3: I'm dishonoring my heritage.

As you downsize, you may want to part with belongings that a family member set aside for you or that someone specifically asked you to keep. This can be especially scary if you feel that items weren't so much given to you as *entrusted* to you. To let them go is to betray that trust, right?

Many people fear that they're going to dishonor their family members, either living or dead, with their choices. But this isn't a fear—it's a form of guilt that plays unfairly with your emotions. Reframe this feeling by acknowledging that you have a chance to discover who you are in relation to these people. In this way, you can reinforce the memory and legacy of those who came before you.

If you could talk to your parents, grandparents, and more distant ancestors, would they say that the most important thing they ever did was collect *stuff*? Ideally, the answer is no.

Also, someone who loves you (or loved you when they were here) wouldn't want you to agonize over a sideboard, a silver tray, or other material things. And if they do, that's not love. It's emotional blackmail. Those who came before you gave you life, and with it the intelligence and free will to make your own decisions. I hope they also showed you how to make decisions that bring joy and happiness, not a crushing sense of obligation to items that were never yours to begin with.

If any of these people are still around, *ask* them what they'd like you to do with their stuff—with the caveat that you will have final decision-making power once it's yours. Odds are very good that they'll tell you to do with it what makes you happy, without added guilt.

Then ask them how they'd like you to honor their legacy in a way that *doesn't* involve their stuff. What values, morals, or other meaningful qualities do they want to live within you and their other descendants? Learning these wishes is a priceless gift of downsizing. So elevate your discussion above physical things to how best to immortalize the people you love and cherish.

Reframing tip: Your home should not be a safety deposit box for your family history, unless that's a choice you deliberately

DIGITAL DOWNSIZING

The digital age means never having to completely lose a possession. If you feel that an object doesn't meet the "treasure" definition, but you need just a little of the memory jog it provides, take a digital picture of it or scan it into your computer. Upload it to the Cloud, and you can access it wherever you go.

If you don't have the time or know-how to upload photos or scan ticket stubs or other memorabilia, perhaps a loved one who's participating in the downsizing can pick up this task.

make. If you choose to take on that responsibility, make sure you have the resources and the enthusiasm to follow through. If you don't, pass your important family-history heirlooms on to someone who does.

#4: I'll disrupt my family's status quo.

Are you afraid that your downsizing is going to permanently change your family in some way?

The truth is, the underlying situation that's prompting your downsizing event may indeed affect your family. But I suspect that these circumstances are either entirely out of your control (job loss, death of parents) or were a reasonable course of events for you to put into motion (retirement, better job, marriage).

So yes, your family may see some changes. But any collection of people, along with the relationships between them, is constantly changing. On some days, they change more than others!

If you're afraid that you're going to fracture your family or permanently injure a relationship, this is an anxiety. Change is

(continued on page 140)

Contrasting Parents Lead to Different Downsizing Trials for Daughter

Meg Lightbown's experience with her family's possessions provides an interesting question. But first, some background.

During a 2-year period in her late twenties, Meg lost both parents. Each went without warning. She hadn't spoken in years with her mother, who struggled with hoarding behaviors and other challenges. Her father, who had raised her since she was 9, "was my best friend," she says.

My question to you is this: When Meg cleared out both their homes, whose stuff created more emotional challenges?

If you answered her mother's, you are . . . correct.

When Meg stepped into her mother's one-bedroom apartment, the sudden exposure to her life came as a shock. "There was a lot of stuff in a very small area. She couldn't just have one thing—she might have 10 bottles of air freshener," recalls Meg, now 34. "It was very difficult to go in there and see all that. It was like she put the stuff around her instead of focusing on her relationship with me."

As she started noticing individual items, Meg found she was more like her mother than she'd realized. "I was like, 'I have this, too! I use this! I like that!' It was giving me the feeling of 'I have a relationship with my mother through the stuff.' I think that's why I kept a lot. I was trying to substitute for the relationship we didn't have."

She drove carloads of her mom's belongings 450 miles back to her home in northern Maine: clothes, inspirational plaques, food ("I like asparagus, she liked asparagus"), candles, and other bric-a-brac. Also, a diabetic cat that needed shots three times daily.

But over time, she found that "When I had it in my house, I didn't feel good about it. One sign said 'Bloom where you're planted.' I put it up in my kitchen, and every time I saw it, I felt bad. Why couldn't she bloom where *she* was planted? You don't want to feel like that. Eventually, over time, I passed the stuff on to charity or other family members," she says.

Her father's home was a different story, even though it was cluttered, too. "I was so secure with my relationship with my dad, and I have such good memories of him. His stuff was just *stuff*."

Years later, only a small number of items from her parents remain. She has journals that her mother wrote in and some pictures of herself she found in her apartment. Her father, a social worker, collected barometers. Meg now displays one in every room of her house. (Her husband, Rob, is happy to look at them. He's a meteorologist.)

"Just thinking of having all that stuff still here, it would have held me back. If you keep the old stuff, you let it define who you are, and you continue to live in the past! I feel like it drags you down if you constantly revisit that past. I want to keep things that just make me feel good," she says.

"I wouldn't wish downsizing on anybody. It was crazy. I think the best thing you can do is keep your possessions to a number that if you were to die tomorrow and someone came in, they could deal with it. They wouldn't be overwhelmed."

often difficult and sometimes painful, but without change, growth would be impossible. It's the unknown here that's causing your anxiety. That's completely normal.

Reframe your anxiety by telling yourself that you're now deliberately reconnecting with your family and rejuvenating your most important relationships.

You've been picking up ideas for making collaborative decisions about family possessions, and you'll learn a lot more in the next section. You're going to have meaningful conversations that will likely reveal unfamiliar facets in your spouse, adult children, parents, and other family members. This understanding creates stronger, more-authentic connections.

With this knowledge, your decisions will be less likely to cause damage and hurt feelings compared to downsizers who make choices that are self-serving, hasty, and poorly informed.

Of course, some people just won't be pleased with any decision that they don't get to make completely on their own. If you're considerate of your loved ones' needs and wishes, play fair, and act in good faith, but they're still unhappy, remember this: Letting go means allowing other people to have their own responses, then giving them time to work through it on their own schedule.

Reframing tip: You can't control how another person will react—but you can be confident that you've done the best you possibly can, while operating from a true and honest place.

#5: I'm scared about my mortality.

Earlier in your journey, your life was neatly divided into small chunks, roughly 5 years for grade school, 3 for middle school, and 4 apiece for high school and college.

But from your early twenties onward, you may not have had many friendly little reminders that you're getting older . . . until

Real-World Downsizing Discovery

Rebecca says: My mom's mother passed away in 1961 at the age of 48. I have vivid childhood memories of my mom still trying to part with her personal belongings. I have always felt that my mom weighed herself down with so much emotional baggage by not shedding these things much earlier. My mom went to work the night her mother passed, and I think she felt quite a bit of guilt for not being there for her dad when he received the news from the hospital. In a way, her inability to move forward from all this heaviness and all of her mom's belongings shortened her own life. Better to keep the wonderful memories of a loved one in your heart and head than in the attic.

---

you downsize. Then a new job (or loss of a job) or a newly empty nest causes you to wonder, *"How did this happen? I swear I was 30 the last time I checked!"*

Two of the more likely reasons why you might be reading this book are because you're retiring or your parent is ailing. Both of these events *really* raise your fear of aging and death.

This fear is actually a form of sadness. Here's a reframing approach that will help you think about it a little differently: This downsizing is a wake-up call that will make you more aware and engaged in the next phase of your life.

Too many people sleepwalk through their days, worrying about the future and regretting the past. As they fantasize and catastrophize, they're missing vast swaths of their real lives, which are going on without them. Surrounding yourself with meaningless clutter further blocks out the real world and further impedes you from being *in* your life.

You now have a marker that serves as the starting point of a new life, which can be just as meaningful and exciting as your high-school graduation.

If anything's dying, let it be your old fears and worries. Let your daydreams and your "what-ifs" and "should-haves" succumb to their mortality. Pack up the possessions that are meaningful to you, and go have an adventure!

While you're at it, also use this next phase to strengthen your legacy among your loved ones. How will you be remembered? Be honest. If your kids and grandkids are going to scratch their heads trying to recall what was really important to you, now's the time to show them. Now's the time to create the kind of memories that you want to live on after you're gone . . . which will be a long time from now . . . but you're not worried about it because you have more life to enjoy.

Reframing tip: There's no easy way to say this, but here goes: You're going to die. We all will. So get over it! In the words of a great Hollywood film, you can get busy living or you can get busy dying. *Downsizing* well will help you *live* well.

#6: I'm afraid that my life has been meaningless.

All people have a moment when they stop, look around, and wonder about the meaning of life—and whether their life has it. If, in the middle of downsizing, this happens to you, then welcome to your moment of existential reflection. I'd be surprised if you *didn't* have such a moment.

Be careful! This experience can evoke a sense of sadness that's similar to the heavy thoughts you might feel when pondering your mortality. So reframing it requires a similar change in your thought process.

It's normal at downsizing milestones to feel like you haven't accomplished enough. These feelings are especially common when your career is coming to a close or you're thinking about the declining vitality or death of a parent whose accomplishments seem bigger than yours.

Reframe this sadness so that you're looking at this turning point as a fresh chance to achieve something that *does* feel meaningful. Give thought to your old goals. Do you still want to achieve them? Are they even achievable now? If your answer to either question is no, let these goals go. They are now as heavy and unusable to you as all the physical possessions you don't need. But if your answer is yes, then make them happen!

Here is your opportunity to create new goals, too. Make sure that they'll be possible in your new environment and with the new resources you'll have at hand.

Whatever has kept you from attaining the meaning you want in your life—whether it's your attitude, a possession, or a sabotaging person—leave it behind in this move.

On a similar note, if you've been overly wrapped up in the *stuff* you own, I guarantee that your life has less meaning than if you had spent your time on learning, loved ones, profound experiences, and helping others. With this downsizing, let stuff go and fill the empty space with these ingredients.

Reframing tip: If you're asking fundamental questions about the meaning of your life, it tells me that you're serious about taking the right steps to ensure that the next phase of your life is the best it can be. Don't let this moment make you sad—get started on making a change!

#7: I'm scared that I'll discard something I'll need later.

I've already discussed the all-too-common concern that you might get rid of an irreplaceable memento, heirloom, or other treasure, then want it back. Here's a related worry: You might let go of a useful item that you'll actually need someday, whether it's a tennis ball, remote control, or pair of pants.

This is also a type of anxiety, and it's one that's easily reframed. Remind yourself that during the *Let It Go* downsizing process, you'll take ample time to ensure that you're surrounding yourself with only the things you truly need.

These useful, functional items aren't treasures, but they aren't trash, either. They fall into the category of potential I-Might-Need-It Items that you'll be deciding whether to take or leave behind. I'll provide more guidelines in the next section to help you make the right decisions about these items.

Still, you might part with something that you later need. It happens. But it's not the end of the world. Borrow the thing from your new friends or neighbors. Buy another one. Or do without it. If it's an expensive tool, rent it for the day, or hire someone who owns the tool to do the job for you. If that day comes, you will find a solution. It will be okay. Don't let this anxiety about an imagined future that may never occur distract you from making smart, informed decisions that make sense to you today.

Reframing tip: Keep in mind that if you've created the home and life you want, and you're surrounded with the things that bring you joy and happiness, being without one useful item someday won't be the end of the world!

#8: I'm scared of the emotional turmoil I'll feel during this process.

I can guarantee that some part of this downsizing will be emotional. How can it not be?

It's very possible that you have stuff down in the murky depths of your mind that you'd prefer not to think about. We all do. That's a big reason why people distract themselves with their smartphones and their streaming television binge-a-thons. It's why they acquire stuff and pile it around themselves. These activities protect you. They allow you to cover up the threatening emotions deep inside. They even act as a shield against reality.

The fear of having to confront whatever's lurking down there is an anxiety. Dig down into your buried memories and emotions and reframe this anxiety. The *Let It Go* way is already preparing you to find the calm that's waiting for you on the other side of this downsizing. Working through your emotions is a normal and healthy part of getting there. Accept it! Embrace it!

Read the extended profiles of the people throughout this book who have successfully downsized (like Meg's story on page 138). Some of them have been through painful struggles. Several became very emotional as they shared their stories with me. But the pain they endured during their downsizing-related events came with solutions to their hurt, as well as an improved ability to grab the fresh opportunities that awaited them.

It's okay to envision the emotional turmoil that may occur as you downsize. But give yourself the chance to also look past it to the rewards you'll enjoy afterward. The upheaval you're dealing with will be short-lived. The gift it's offering will last forever.

Reframing tip: Remember that change is frightening, and the only way over it is through it. One way or another, you're going to get through this downsizing milestone. You might as well do it calmly and purposefully.

#9: I'm afraid of damaging the planet.

This is a fear—more accurately, a sense of guilt—that people often describe to me. They worry that their downsizing will create yet more garbage. If this one's bothering you, let me help you think about it a little differently.

This downsizing move is an opportunity for you to help as many of your possessions as possible find a new life. It's never been easier to put vintage clothes, pop-culture memorabilia, books, well-loved furniture, and other items into the hands of someone who will use and appreciate them. Advertise them on Craigslist, eBay, or The Freecycle Network. List them in your employee newsletter or donate them to your church or a local thrift store.

For as much as Americans throw away (more than 260 million tons went into landfills in one recent year, according to a 2015 study), our nation also creates an abundance of crafty individuals who enjoy reusing and recycling. Jot down on a sticky note how much you loved and used this object. Or write instructions on how to turn this item into something new, courtesy of Pinterest. Attach the note and let the thing go on to make its next owner happy. (And I do mean let it go. Worrying about what the next person will do with it is a weight that you don't need and shouldn't accept.)

Reframing tip: If you're having trouble shaking your guilt, do something good to balance the scales. Plant some trees. Donate a little more to an environmental organization. Pick up some trash from your new community, or volunteer a few extra hours for an organization that improves our society.

In the past two sections, I've been helping you get mentally and emotionally ready for your downsizing process. (If you've been exercising to prepare for the *physical* challenge of downsizing, congratulations!)

The preparation period has now come to an end. In the next section, you'll put all that planning into action!

LET IT GO EXERCISE 6:
Explore Your Downsizing Fears

Today, think about whether the idea of getting rid of any of your possessions makes you feel any of the common downsizing fears. Then trace those fears back to see if they lead to any sadness, anger, or guilt.

If you plan on keeping these items, is it solely because you're feeling a SAG emotion? What steps can you take to let these items go—along with the emotions that are attached to them?

Emotion	Items That Create It	Steps I Can Take to Let These Go
SADNESS		
ANXIETY		
GUILT		

PART THREE

It's Time to Downsize

We've now reached a fork in the road.

Thus far, I've been showing you the basics of how to downsize thoroughly, which means working through the possessions in your home, the burdens cluttering your mind, and the connections between them. This is stuff that *everyone* needs to know, regardless of why they're downsizing.

With these tools, you'll be able to work with more speed and less distress when it's time to sort your stuff into "keep" and "let it go" piles.

And that time has arrived!

To proceed, please choose the correct chapter for your downsizing situation.

- If you're downsizing your *own* home, continue to Chapter 7.

- If you're downsizing your *parents'* home, skip to Chapter 8.

- If you're downsizing anyone else's home, such as a close friend or other family member who has departed, Chapter 8 will provide the best directions to follow.

If any information is useful for both scenarios, I've included it in both places, so you won't miss anything by focusing on just one chapter.

CHAPTER 7

Downsizing Your Own Home

ello there! How are you feeling today? Are you well rested? Energetic? Does this feel like a good day to start sorting through your things and packing boxes?

I hope so!

You're about to scan your eyes across all your possessions, then decide their fate: What do I keep? What do I let go? If a disruptive emotion flares up, you'll deal with it, let it go, and move on. Before you joined me, this downsizing might have felt like a final exam that you weren't prepared to take.

But now, it'll hopefully feel like a pop quiz on a familiar topic. Actually, you already have a *lot* of the answers!

At times, I'll ask you to go back and gather your responses that you jotted down in the exercises in the first half of the book. These will help you make your decisions more quickly and efficiently.

The flowchart on page 189 will direct the actions you'll take. In the first step, you'll pick out the most important possessions that you'll take with you on your journey: the items I call your treasures. Next, you'll choose a sensible number of "worthy" items to bring with you because you still need and use them, and they fit well in your new space. That's all you'll be keeping—treasures and worthy items. But your important decisions aren't finished.

You'll then figure out what to do with the stuff that you're leaving behind. Do you sell it, give it away, or throw it away? The right choices can add to your happiness and maybe your bank account. The flowchart will walk you through your options so that each step is as efficient and rewarding as possible.

The downsizing experience that begins today is just going to be a little blip on your timeline, and before you know it, you'll be enjoying the next stage of your life.

You're now a downsizing machine! You're built to succeed, you're fueled up, and you're ready to begin.

So push the start button, and let's go!

STEPS 1 AND 2: DEFINE YOUR TREASURES AND GIVE THEM THE DINING ROOM TABLE TEST

You'll be sorting through:

☐ MEMORY ITEMS

Treasures   Forgotten items

Trinkets   Malignant items

Your first step is to set aside the treasures you need to bring. Note that I say *need* rather than *want*. These are the must-have items that mark the highlights of your life or your family's life and deserve to be remembered. If you could read your story like a tree's, these would be the rings that mark the best, most important, and greatest moments.

So identify them now. Once these are accounted for, I guarantee that you'll feel less stressed about your downsizing. As a result, the rest of the process will probably go even more easily.

Did you complete the "Making My Treasure Map" exercise on page 93? If so, pull out this list and collect the items on it. These will probably make up a lot of the treasures you'll take. If you haven't done this exercise, please do so now.

Another place where you'll find possible treasures is from the "The Objects That Identify Me" exercise you did on page 53. Some of the best moments in your life may have been linked to an activity or role that was important to your identity, such as working professional, mom, or amateur bobsledding champion. Go back and look at that list or complete it if you skipped over it the first time. If any of these items rank among your "mosts, bests, and greatests," pull them out and set them aside.

As you go around the house retrieving treasures, place them on your dining room table. As I mentioned earlier, the Dining Room Table Test determines how many treasures you can take. When your table is full, you've maxed out your quota of treasures!

If you have too many items for your table to hold, ask yourself if you have defined your treasures too broadly. If you don't make the effort to find the true, streamlined "best-of" treasures at this stage, you'll be sabotaging yourself and the whole downsizing process.

I understand that there are some variables in these steps that may require some explanation or beg some further questions.

Q. How many leaves can I put into my table to give myself more room?

Nice try. If you are looking for this type of leeway, I'm inclined to ask how seriously you are taking this process! While the Dining Room Table Test is completely arbitrary—I'm the first to admit that—you have to set a limit, or you'll be in trouble fast. In my experience, the size of this table is proportional to the size of the rooms in your home. Don't look for ways to cheat—look for ways to find only the best treasures!

Q. Does everyone in the home have to fit their treasures onto one table?

That's up to you to decide. Are we just talking about you and your spouse? I think in many cases, two people can reasonably fit their treasures on a decent-size dining room table. But it's okay for each of you to get your own table, if necessary, especially if it's a particularly small table.

If you have one or more kids, I certainly don't expect the family to share one table for their treasures. However, I don't think each child warrants as much space as an adult should have. Carefully monitor what goes into your kids' treasure piles. Often *everything* is a treasure to a child, including the stuff they'd quickly forget if they no longer had it.

The point here is to establish a very clear limit for you, your kids, and your spouse. (Though when I was downsizing my parents' home, it's worth noting that the treasures my six siblings and I chose didn't even fill the table!)

Q. Can you come help me lift this sofa/hope chest/riding lawnmower onto my table? It's heavy!

Sorry, I'm just here to offer advice and encouragement! I can show you how to successfully downsize, but the heavy lifting is up to you.

If you have furniture that you consider a treasure, you can exempt it from the table test. Consider it a freebie that doesn't count against your quota.

But before you pledge to wheel it into the moving truck and ship it across town, the state, or the country, ask yourself, *"Why would I really be keeping this thing?"* As I've already mentioned, and an outside expert will confirm later in this chapter, you're likely never going to sell heavy, old furniture for any appreciable amount of money. If a knowledgeable appraiser has told you—recently . . . not in 1991!—that your sofa is worth a lot of money, that's one thing. But if you're operating on wishful thinking, that's another.

Do you want to keep the sofa or the memory attached to it? (This is always a good question to ask, even if the object is a small trinket.)

Do you want this sofa only because your parents treasured it and you're supposed to pass it along to your kids? Take a close look at your feelings. Do you truly enjoy this sofa? Do you actually use it? Is it comfortable? Will it look good in your new home? Do you have the space for it? (And I'm not talking about putting it in your garage until you can work something out.) If so, then keep it!

On the other hand, is the cost to move the sofa more than it's actually worth? If so, I think you know what to do.

Is it uncomfortable, awkward, and saggy? Don't keep it! Also, don't keep it just because someone told you it was an heirloom. You're an adult, and this couch is now yours. *You* get to decide what an heirloom is in your family. Odds are good that your Gen X or millennial offspring won't want this thing when it's their turn to receive it. If this couch— or whatever large object you're looking at—no longer has a place in your family's life, don't pass it and the guilt on to your kids. Let it end here.

Now let's talk about the hope chest. Every family has some equivalent of this. It might be a sideboard filled with linens that belonged to your grandmother, a cabinet that holds stuff collected during family trips when you were a child, or an actual chest at the foot of your bed that contains seldom-looked-at family keepsakes. If you have such a container filled with items that you just *know* are treasures, open it and go through these items one by one. Each must bring up a memory of a "most, best, or greatest" moment in your life. As I'm sure you'll find out, the entire contents of the container *won't* meet these criteria.

As far as the lawnmower goes, if it's something you use regularly and you'll have room for it at your next home, consider it a "worthy" item even if it also has sentimental value. These are belongings that are important to you because you often *need* them. Your hair dryer, television, and toaster also fall into this category. Ignore these for now. You'll judge them later by a different set of criteria.

Q. *The vintage sausage grinders/medical books/office equipment that help me remember my father's hard work take up a lot of space on the table!*

Remember, you're keeping the *best item*, not the *best category*. One of those sausage grinders touches your heart in a particular way. Maybe it's the one with the handle that's more worn down from your father's hand. Maybe the best book from your father's medical practice is the one with the most notes he doodled in the margins, or it's the one you remember him pulling off the shelf to help you answer a science question in 11th grade.

You don't need *everything* if you have the *one best thing*. Focus all your love, gratitude, and pride for this aspect of your loved one into this singular thing. Downsizing means using a little flash drive to store your memories—not a supercomputer.

Q. *What if some of my "mosts, bests, and greatests" list of treasures kind of bums me out?*

Some of the items linked to our important moments bring up a mix of emotions, like the things that remind us of people we've lost or the hard times we've endured.

If that memento of your late mother brings up grief every time you look at it, then the difficult truth is that it's time to get rid of it so you won't look at it anymore. This is a malignant item—not a treasure. Instead, keep a different item that helps you remember her in a way that feels better to you.

Objects have the power to immediately return us to a certain time and place. This can be a happy experience that we enjoy reminiscing about or a sad one that evokes memories we'd rather forget. You have a choice over which you'll remember.

Dig deeper so you can hear the precise message that this hurtful object is telling you. Is it time to talk to a professional with a background in grief counseling so you can work through your feelings?

Also, when you see evidence of an adversity you overcame, if your feelings are more bitter than sweet, let this item go. It, too, is malignant. I've noticed that people sometimes keep medical equipment after an illness or surgery *way* longer than they should. On the one hand, these objects are a testament to a trauma that they've overcome, but it's also possible that these things keep jabbing at an emotionally sore spot for no good reason.

If you have an item that reminds you how you rose phoenix-like to become stronger than ever, then keep it. It's a treasure. If it just reminds you that you got really, really sick once, then let it go. It's malignant.

Q. A lot of my stuff is still necessary for an element of my identity. Do I have to pick out only the best?

No. If you're still a working professional, keep the gear you regularly use. If you're still a bobsledder, keep your bobsled.

These things aren't treasures—they're worthy items.

On the other hand, if you have a formerly worthy item linked to an important part of your identity from the *past*, or that you think will someday help your loved ones recall a "most, best, or greatest" about you, then consider whether it could be a treasure. (This could be, perhaps, the calculator you used in accounting school or the backpack you carried when you were a Scout leader.)

STEP 3: DEFINE YOUR WORTHY ITEMS

You'll be sorting through:

☐ I-MIGHT-NEED-IT ITEMS

Worthy items	Items that might be worthy to someone else

Most likely, your I-Might-Need-It Items feel pretty important to you, but they're not glued to you with powerful emotional bonds like your Memory Items. So in one regard, if it's time to leave these behind, you can probably do so more easily. On the other hand, you have a lot more of these items, so this step may take more time.

The I-Might-Need-It Items are things that are useful to *someone*, whether that's you, a family member, a friend, or a stranger. The worthy items are things within this category that you'll keep, so long as you use them regularly and have space for them in your new home. The rest of the I-Might-Need-It Items will go . . . somewhere else. We'll get back to them later.

As you judge the worthiness of the items in your home, ask yourself: *"Is this thing useful enough to warrant the space it will require?"* My guess is that your socks and underwear will meet this benchmark, and likely your silverware, suits, ties, and basic home-repair tools will, too. If your new home has a guest suite, perhaps you should bring your extra set of bath towels, even if you don't use them much now. If you're moving to a studio apartment with very limited space, then you probably should leave them behind. (I'll help you figure out the limitations of the space in your new home in the next step.)

Here are some common unconvincing justifications that people use for keeping items that aren't really worthy.

"This is worthy because it was expensive." The price you paid for an object should not determine its importance in your new space. I often tell people that if a low price is the only reason that you want to buy an item, you shouldn't buy it. When it comes to downsizing, you can turn that advice on its head: If a high price is the only reason why you want to keep an item, you shouldn't keep it.

Instead, a worthy item's significance comes from whether:

- It will help you create the home and the life you want
- It's something you'll use regularly and enjoy
- It fits into the space you've allocated for it in your new home

"This is worthy because it'll be a good backup." A downsized home leaves little, if any, room for duplicates. If you anticipate that one item might break down, why not have a backup for *all* the items you own? It won't work. You simply can't downsize while awaiting a bunch of worst-case scenarios.

Bring what you know you'll need *when you arrive,* and don't worry so much about making contingency plans that require you to hold extra items on standby.

"This is worthy because I might need it sometime." This is similar to the "backup" criteria above—and it's also a nonstarter. Please *do* prepare for potentially serious events that could reasonably happen. That's why people keep a fire extinguisher in the kitchen and a blanket in the car trunk.

But *don't* overstock in anticipation of every unlikely situation that might create a minor inconvenience. Instead, make sensible choices that fit within your new home's space and will support the day-to-day life you'll be living.

If you're selling your car to live in a walking-friendly retirement community with a shuttle service, you don't need to keep your jumper cables.

"This is worthy because someone gave it to me as a gift." If it's a gift that you love, use, and have space to keep, then take it with you. If it's a gift that you only want to take in case Aunt Lucy stops by and asks where the hand-carved back scratcher went, then *don't* keep it. It's time to step up and create the home *you* want, not a home filled with guilt or emotional drama.

"This is worthy because it looks terrific in my home." Remember that you're not going to be living in this home much longer. Will this piece of decor truly match the design of your new place? If you already know that it won't, there's no need to take it with you just to prove later that you were right.

"This is worthy because I don't feel like going through this stuff and evaluating all of it." Items go into the "worthy" category because they're useful and functional—and determining these qualities sometimes takes effort. You may have to put batteries in a gadget to see if it still works, inflate the air mattresses to make sure they don't leak, and try on clothes to see if they fit.

Yes, this takes time. But it also takes time to load and unload these things, it costs money to move them, and it requires effort to try them out in your new home and toss them when they don't meet your needs. Just take the moment to check them now.

"This is worthy because my adult kids might need it." My suggestion is to offer this item to your kids, instead of making assumptions about what they need. (And consider letting them "shop" around your house and request items you didn't realize they needed.)

WOULD YOU PAY FOR
THIS OLD ITEM AGAIN?

If you're paying for movers, always think about the cost of each do-I-keep-this-or-let-it-go decision.

I have heard many times from moving professionals that the cost of relocating items is often far greater than their actual value. If someone took your old loveseat, faded rug, or forgotten box in your basement and told you that you'd have to pay cash to get it back, would you pay the ransom?

If not, why would you pay to move these things to your new home?

Your home is not a storage facility. Nor are you a porter carrying supplies for a mountain expedition. If your grown kids don't need it now or aren't prepared to take it now, then that's the end of the discussion. The item is not worthy.

"This is worthy because of the memory attached to it." *Everything* you own has a memory attached to it. Even if an item has a powerful memory linked to it, that alone is not a sufficient reason to keep it. If a functional item happens to be a treasure (it captures a "best, most, or greatest" from your life), then it gets to go with you because it's a treasure. If not, then acknowledge the strong memory, take a photo of the object if it'll help make you feel better, and then let it go. You'll make wonderful new memories in your new home.

For the I-Might-Need-It Items that don't make the cut to go with you, ask yourself another question: Would anyone else possibly want this thing? Would a stranger buy this if you sold it at a garage sale? Would you feel like you were making the world a better place if you dropped this off at a donation center? If the answer to any of these questions is no, the item is likely trash that you will eventually need to throw away or recycle.

Right now, though, just separate the I-Might-Need-It Items into two piles: what you'll bring with you and what you'll let go. Once you've done that, you can move on to the next step, which is to figure out whether the treasures and worthy items you want to take will actually fit into your new home.

STEP 4: DO YOUR SPACE AUDIT

You'll be evaluating whether you indeed have space for your:

Treasures   Worthy items

Creating a space you love within your new home is not unlike beginning a relationship with someone new. You have to honor and respect that home from the very start, just like you would the relationship, if it's going to be satisfying and sustainable.

If you don't treat your new home with that honor and respect—if you overload it and push its boundaries—you can never be happy in that space, just like your relationship will be unhappy if you trample over the other person's limits (which shows neither honor nor respect).

To learn your new home's boundaries, give it a space audit. Doing a space audit means measuring your new home's rooms in a specific way so you can better understand how much you can bring.

Below is the method I use. The last time I moved, I was able to unpack and put away almost all of our belongings before the movers left, so they could take most of the moving boxes with them. Talk about starting your new life in a calm, uncluttered space!

You already know which treasures and worthy items you want to bring with you. The space audit is a way of double-checking that they'll fit, while you still have time to jettison items, if necessary. The audit will also help you plan where you'll unload your boxes, which will make move-in day easier. Here's how to do it.

Think of your new home as a collection of spaces. Thinking *"I'll move this to my new home"* is an overly broad and general statement that discourages downsizing. So I recommend *shrinking* your *thinking*.

This means viewing your new home not as one space, but as many smaller individual spaces, each of which will be used for a specific purpose. Not only should you break your new home into rooms but you should also consider the spaces within each room.

You may have:

- A space for your kitchen appliances
- A space in the hallway closet for your bath towels
- A space on the built-in bookshelf in the living room for your books

This is a bit like planning a week's worth of meals before you go shopping. If you just throw food into one big space—your shopping cart—you may buy too much of one thing and not enough of another. You also might not have enough room in your pantry or freezer when you get home. Instead, envision the cart as 21 small spaces that you need to fill with components for 21 meals, and your shopping trip will be more efficient, with less potential for overcrowding and waste. That's what you want with your downsizing, too!

Assess your new spaces. While you're visiting your new home before your move, walk through the rooms with a tape measure and sketch out all the spaces on paper (plain or graph). Essentially, you're making a rough blueprint of the home.

Include the storage or display space that you have available in each room. Be as specific as you can in identifying these spaces ("two 4-foot-by-8-foot walk-in closets in the master bedroom; four shelves in the living room measuring 18 inches by 12 inches by 10 inches; four kitchen drawers measuring 18 inches by 12 inches by 5 inches"). Also note the size of open wall areas and the position of doors and windows so you have a sense of where artwork and bookcases, sideboards, or other storage units might comfortably fit in your new home.

If possible, photograph each room thoroughly to supplement your sketches. One method I use is to stand in the center of a room and take four photos, one of each wall. Be sure that closet and cabinet doors are open so that you can get a visual sense of their internal size.

Print out the photos of each room and put them together with your sketch of the house. You have now completed your space audit, and you know the total available space you have for your possessions. You can stop short of filling all the space if you wish (and I'd applaud you for that), but you absolutely, positively can't *overfill* it!

If you're in the challenging position of moving to a home that you haven't actually visited in person, ask a helpful party—such as a real estate agent, property manager, landlord, or current owner of the home—to provide blueprints, measurements, and photos of each room as I've described.

Tell yourself if it doesn't fit, it doesn't come with you. If it's becoming clear that you have too much stuff for your new home, now is the time to reduce the volume until you're within your space constraints. This is your last chance to ensure that you've meaningfully downsized.

You only have the space you have. This is worth repeating, since it's so important: *You only have the space you have!* You can argue its truth or wish it were otherwise, but at some stage, you have to face it. Accept this fact now, or you'll struggle with it later.

Every choice you've made during this process either increased or decreased the amount of stuff that you'll bring. Your "material convoy" is flexible—you can make it larger or smaller. However, the space available to you in your new home is fixed.

In other words, you never have *too little space*! If you ever feel this way, the problem is actually that you have *too much stuff*. If your space audit reveals that your stuff isn't going to fit, keep sorting through your possessions, shedding the things that are least important to your happiness or your daily life, until what you're taking will fit comfortably into the spaces that you've sketched, photographed, and measured.

Having done the audit, pack for the spaces that await you. Now comes another challenging part (but a *fun* challenge)! As you begin to pack items for the move, decide now which room and which space those items will go into. Clearly envision, with as much detail as possible, how each space will look. If you don't picture a reasonable place for your stuff to go— especially the large items—reconsider whether you should bring them.

You might pack one box for the cupboard in the kitchen that will hold baking supplies, two boxes for the bookshelf in your bedroom, and three feet of hanging items that will easily fit into your closet. This will take discipline and focus. But you'll be minimizing the chance for complications when you later unpack.

To make the unpacking process even easier, label each moving box with its contents and its assigned room. This way, anyone assisting with your move can locate where things belong and place them there with ease.

If this space audit process feels unnecessarily painstaking, I'd ask you to consider this: Would you take your family on a vacation and not check first to ensure that there will be enough beds for everyone? That would be a sure way to ruin your holiday before it even begins. So why does it make sense to move to a new home without first determining if there's adequate space for everything you're taking with you?

The principles of honor and respect for your new home that I spoke of earlier require that you treat it well and help it become the backdrop for the next happy phase of your life.

EXTRA STEP—PLAN AHEAD AND MAKE YOUR WISHES KNOWN

On the flowchart on page 189 that guides you through your downsizing process, you'll see an extra step set off by itself: Tell other people where you want your stuff to go after you're gone.

This task is not necessarily important for *this particular* downsizing. But it's absolutely crucial that you do it sooner rather than later. If you have time to do it now, do it now. If not, then do it as soon as possible after you finish your downsizing-related move.

A recent survey found that nearly two-thirds of Americans don't have a will. Among Americans with children, 55 percent don't have this vital document.

People in their twenties, thirties, and early forties are especially unlikely to have a will. I suspect that it's because it takes time to do estate planning, and when you're young, you tend to think you'll live forever. If you want to ensure that all the i's are dotted and t's are crossed, it also takes money to hire a lawyer with the expertise to write the will. That said, the time, effort, and money are definitely worth the peace of mind it brings.

But I'd venture to say that the main reason why people may

find estate planning even less appealing than downsizing is because it makes them think about their deaths. More specifically, it requires thinking about your loved ones coping with your death, which is its own special flavor of unpleasant. So it's easier *not* to do this planning and let your fear of dying smolder quietly on some deep level.

It's time to dig down and confront your mortality. Reframe this fear so it becomes a precious gift that you give your family.

Look, you're going to die whether or not you do this planning (and I'm fairly certain that writing your will won't make you die *sooner*). After you're gone, don't you want your loved ones to say, "We sure are glad that Dad and Mom were smart and caring enough to let us know their wishes in advance! We don't have to figure this out on our own, or perhaps even worse, have to follow a court's decision."

The way you live your life (including the choices you make to keep or let go of possessions) helps create your legacy. Maybe you've worked hard, saved and invested your money well, and built up valuable assets to leave to your spouse, kids, and grandkids so their lives will be a little easier. Or maybe you won't be able to leave them as much stuff with monetary value, but you hope to set an example of how to live a caring and thoughtful life. Maybe you want your property *and* your good example to create your legacy.

So make sure your physical possessions—and everything else of value, like investments and life insurance—will be distributed the way you want after you're gone. While you're at it, make your wishes known about how *you* want to be cared for if you can't speak for yourself.

You can do these things by having honest conversations with your loved ones, as well as by creating and updating several key legal documents.

Talk with Your Family

If your adult children or other loved ones are gathering to help you with a later-in-life downsizing, consider whether you want to pass along some of your family heirlooms and prized possessions now.

If you're not ready to give them up now—or they're not ready to take them—perhaps you can have a conversation about where you want these items to go. If you don't want to pick a specific recipient, let your kids know which items are special enough that you hope they stay in the family, and let them work together to call dibs on the items in advance. You might want to mark items with a little hidden tag with the name of the recipient, jot it down in a notebook, or both. (It may also be a good idea to provide this information in your will.)

If your kids don't want your treasures, don't try to guilt them into taking them. These things are important to *you*. They mark *your* happy memories, *your* identity, and *your* accomplishments. These may not be a meaningful way that your children would choose to remember you. Furthermore, your kids don't *have* to have a reason for not wanting your things. They get to choose which items they want in their homes, just like you do.

Offer your possessions in a spirit of generosity, but if your kids (or grandkids or other loved ones) decline them, accept their decision calmly. It's your *stuff* they're rejecting, not you.

Someone whose taste is modern architecture and design may not want your wicker furniture. Your 22-year-old tablet-toting grandson may not want your massive row of encyclopedias. Someone who secretly felt like your career or your hobbies kept you away from home too often may not want objects related to your career or your hobbies.

Or maybe they just don't have the room for it! Remember: They only have the space they have. When they take on too much of someone else's stuff, they can't live their lives fully, either.

Fill Out Your Legal Documents

As you pass through the different stages that require you to downsize, the essentials of your life that you want to protect will change dramatically. In your early twenties, maybe you just have a car and a cat. Maybe you'll get married in the following years and need to provide for your spouse. For a period during your life, you may have kids at home. Along the way, you may pick up a bigger home, a vacation cottage, investments, expensive toys, and grandkids. At all of these times, you also have yourself to think about.

If you get too sick to communicate your needs, you'll want some way to tell your loved ones and your doctors how to take care of you. If you disappear from the picture, you'll want a way to distribute your stuff to the people you care about.

The best way to do this is by maintaining the proper legally valid documents. It's not enough to just create these documents once—even though that's more than a lot of people do. You have to check in periodically to make sure they're up-to-date and accurate. That's because the documents you create in your twenties or thirties may not reflect your circumstances in your forties, fifties, and beyond.

Brian Caverly, a semiretired estate planning attorney in Pennsylvania and coauthor of *Estate Planning for Dummies,* told me that a common problem he sees is that "people will write a will and never change it. People die, they get divorced, and they become estranged from each other. This can be more of a problem than if they had died without a will."

Given that you're downsizing because of a big change in your life, do the details of your important documents need revision? Is a piece of official paper still floating around that specifies your life insurance or home should go to your ex-spouse if you die? Better find out!

Also, did you ever appoint someone to play an important role if you fall into a coma or die, and that person has since died or moved out of your life? Better find out!

"My recommendation is that everyone who comes into my office will leave the office with a will and a durable power of attorney, a health-care power of attorney, and a living will or some type of advanced directive," says Larry Lehmann, an estate attorney in New Orleans who also serves as the president of the National Association of Estate Planners and Councils.

Let's take a look at these documents.

A will. This specifies how you want your property divided after your death. If you have minor children, you can also appoint a guardian to take care of them when you're gone.

These are extremely important choices, and you want to be the one to make them. If you don't create a will, the law of your state will take control, and it may be different than you want for your family. If your will contains errors that render it invalid, the same situation may happen.

Another document that can distribute your property is a living trust. Depending on your needs, you may be able to use a trust instead of a will, or in addition to it. This is something to discuss with your attorney.

If you have a will, you'll need to name an *executor* for it. This is the person who's legally charged with ensuring that the directions in the will are carried out. Responsibilities include dividing up your estate like you wanted and making sure that the estate pays any bills or debts that you owed. If you create a trust, it will need a *trustee*, who has a similar responsibility to carry out your wishes.

Put a great deal of thought into whom you choose as your executor or trustee. This is a big, possibly time-consuming responsibility that requires some basic financial and legal knowledge.

"First thing, you need to choose someone honest and fair, who isn't going to be carrying any grudges and using that position to get even with siblings. I've seen those kinds of situations," Caverly says. "You'll want to have someone who's evenhanded and is going to do what mom or dad wanted. It also helps to have someone with some knowledge of accounting, who can keep records, and who understands the filing requirements for taxes. You'll at least want someone with the capacity to understand what the issues are and who can hire a lawyer or accountant, if necessary."

Sometimes people look to outsiders to take these roles, such as a lawyer or family friend. Depending on your circumstances, you may want to explore this option.

A durable power of attorney. This allows someone you trust—such as your spouse, an adult child, a sibling, or a friend—to step in and make important decisions on your behalf if you become incapacitated. Quite a few illnesses and injuries can leave you in this position, even if you're young.

It's possible to give one person the power to handle different types of health-care and financial decisions. Or you can give one person power of attorney for health matters and someone else power of attorney for money-related issues.

A living will. This is different from the type of will that distributes your property to your loved ones. Among other things, a living will specifies what kind of medical treatment you want at the end of your life. If you require machines to keep you alive, and you're never going to improve, do you want your doctors to step back and just keep you comfortable until the end? Or do you want every treatment in the hospital in order to stay alive as long as possible? This document lets you decide—so someone else doesn't have to.

STEP 5: RETURN OTHER PEOPLE'S STUFF TO THEIR RIGHTFUL OWNERS

You'll be giving back:

> Things that aren't yours

As you downsize your home, it's likely that you'll find things that belong to someone else: stuff you borrowed and never returned, items you've promised to someone and never delivered, and all the things that your kids left behind when they moved out or that you saved for them because you just knew they'd want them one day.

Guess what? Today is that day!

Things That Belong to Someone Else

Even though these items aren't yours, giving them up can be difficult. That's because you may have to make an awkward call to your friend, neighbor, or sibling to admit that you still have their chainsaw or casserole dish. A little humor will undoubtedly help here. (*I only kept this thing so long so I'd have an excuse to call you and chat someday. So here we are!*)

Offer to return the item. If the equivalent of the statute of limitations has expired and they no longer need it, then suggest you'd happily donate it to charity. (Bonus move: If you have another possession that you know this person might want, offer it up as a way of repaying the interest for the thing she loaned you.)

Things You've Been Saving for Your Kids

It's so common for parents to save things for their children that I'm surprised when I'm helping them downsize and they *don't* have boxes of schoolwork and art projects to give their kids when they move into their first apartment or buy their starter home.

I'll share a hard truth with you here: In my experience, saving things that belonged to your children is more likely related to your difficulty admitting that your kids are grown

Real-World Downsizing Discovery

Rose says: After my husband and I got married, my mother-in-law gave him a box of things he left behind at her house. She didn't feel it was her place to just get rid of his "stuff." She gave him more boxes for his birthday and Christmas for quite a few years, wrapped in beautiful paper with a bow. They contained jeans many sizes too small, his coin collection, motorcycle parts, and college memorabilia. We'd create and rehash memories when he opened each box, and we laughed so hard until we cried over the contents.

We kept very little from those gifts—only what meant the most—and we "re-homed" most of the contents. I have shared this story repeatedly over the years with many mothers who wondered what to do with the things their children left behind. Now with both of my girls married with homes of their own, I am continuing the tradition.

and independent than it is about preserving things your kids really need or want.

Also, those toys and toddler books that hold strong emotions and wonderful memories for you may mean little to your grown children. It's time to call your kids and ask them to decide what to do with these things. Give them a deadline to claim what they want, and help them define whether these items are treasures or not.

If your kids don't want these things, and they're still in good condition, could you sell or donate them? If they have no value to anyone else, accept the fact that it's time to throw them away. (As usual, consider taking photos of the things that are most memory-laden. If you'd like, they could make a fun photo book for your kids to look at when they visit.)

Things Someone Has Asked You to Hold

Has anyone left possessions with you to "look after" or "hold on to" for a brief time that turned into years? These items can be a little more difficult to clear from your home, especially if the owner is uncooperative.

In this situation, give a very clear deadline for this ex-neighbor, old roommate, former spouse, or college buddy to come collect this stuff. Be assertive in explaining that you're about to move out and leave these items homeless.

If the owner can't come get them, your options may include shipping them (with reimbursement to you for the cost), putting them in storage locally under the owner's name and with their credit card footing the bill, or donating them to charity if they're not gone by the deadline.

You're not running a storage unit. If the owner of the items doesn't care enough to have them back in his home, there's no reason why you should be saddled with them.

BEFORE THE CALL, PRACTICE YOUR SCRIPT

If your children, friends, ex-neighbors, or distant relatives have been using your basement or garage as storage for too long, here are some lines that you may want to practice before calling them, or modify for an e-mail to send.

"Hi John, your [fill in the blank] has been in the basement for years. We can't store it any longer. If it's still important to you, here are your options:

- *You can come get it in the next 2 weeks.*

- *I can put it into storage, but I'll need your credit card number to ensure that the monthly fee is properly billed to you.*

- *I can have the items shipped to you, but again, I'll need your credit card number to cover the shipping charges.*

- *I can donate what's in the basement.*

- *I can go ahead and throw the items away."*

STEP 6: GIVE TO FAMILY, FRIENDS, AND NEIGHBORS

You'll be evaluating whether you want to share your:

Trinkets	I-Might-Need-It Items that
Forgotten items	you didn't find worthy of keeping

Now it's time to start figuring out what to do with your stuff that you don't want: Memory Items that didn't qualify as treasures and I-Might-Need-It Items that didn't qualify as worthy to you.

What do you want to accomplish with these things that still have some value? If you want to turn it all into as much money as possible, skip to the next step, which is selling it. But you might consider using this opportunity to give gifts to people you know who would appreciate them.

Consider offering useful items to your aunts, uncles, cousins, nieces and nephews, friends, neighbors, and fellow CrossFit participants and worship congregants. Maybe a young person you know who's heading off to college would like some cookware. Maybe an older person who doesn't like newer technology would like your DVD movie collection.

If you're about to move out of the area, distributing some of your possessions will help ensure that your friends and loved ones have reminders of your presence and the stories you shared.

STEP 7: OFFER WORTHWHILE ITEMS FOR SALE

You'll be evaluating how to sell your remaining:

| Trinkets | I-Might-Need-It Items that |
| Forgotten items | you didn't find worthy of keeping |

You have several options if you want to sell your items of value that remain. Choices include a garage sale, an estate sale, or selling the items online.

Before we discuss these options in depth, I'd like to help you develop some realistic expectations about the money you might make. If you are unloading art and antiques, then you may enjoy a windfall when you sell your possessions.

But you may also find that your valuables aren't so, well, *valuable*, warns Julie Hall. She's an estate sale professional and the director of the American Society of Estate Liquidators.

In Chapter 1, I discussed how few people want those huge

wooden TV entertainment centers that were once common in living rooms, and many millennials don't even want a television. I was hoping to prepare you for this moment.

If buyers turn up their nose at your prized possessions, the experience may feel like a painful jolt. Their reaction might feel to you like they're criticizing your sense of style.

If this happens, in some cases, your would-be buyers may simply have homes that aren't suited for what you're selling. "In the Carolinas, we have fabulous historic homes, then you see the older vintage houses from the 1930s and 1940s that are being bulldozed, either to put up a McMansion or a petite, simple midcentury look-alike. There's no dining room. There's no formal living room. It's all an open concept. This is what the thirtysomethings want," Hall says.

Or the collectibles that you thought were valuable may have been at one time, but they aren't anymore. Maybe an object you had appraised years ago has fallen from favor. Maybe the silver market is down. Maybe you've been treasuring family antiques for decades without realizing that "just because it's old doesn't mean it's valuable. They made junk in the 1850s, too," Hall says.

The price of many possessions is also being pushed downward because your potential shoppers can find objects for sale all over the world through their computers and smartphones. "I don't want to point the finger solely at huge online auctions, but when you thought something was rare in your region, go online and suddenly there's 9,432 of them on eBay," Hall says.

So for all those reasons, please keep in mind that generally speaking, you don't have the upper hand in determining the value of your household items. The buyers do. And "what we're seeing now is a significant decline in value and a strong buyer's market," Hall says.

As long as you go into this process with reasonable expectations, the process of selling your property can be a positive experience. You'll probably make at least *some* money. You may also have the opportunity to meet the people who will be providing a new "life" for the belongings that were important to you. But be prepared for the time and effort involved, and decide whether that commitment is going to be worth the return you'll likely have.

Even if you don't meet the buyers—which you may or may not want to do, for reasons you'll see shortly—you'll at least know that some of the objects that you've bought, preserved, looked at, and touched are circulating widely in the world. Even though you're moving on, all these strangers are still valuing the decisions you made long ago.

So let's start looking at how to have the best possible selling experience, starting with garage sales.

Garage Sales: The Do-It-Yourself Approach

Lynda Hammond was rummaging through the items at an older woman's garage sale near Phoenix when she came across a collection of antique clothes irons.

Hammond, a former TV news anchor who still has a love for listening to people's stories, had to learn more. "She grew up with 13 brothers and sisters. Her mother would wake up at 4:00 a.m., and every morning until 6:00 a.m., she'd iron clothing. It was a beautiful way for this woman to start her day quietly. It was a soothing, therapeutic time for her, since at 6, the kids would wake up and all hell would break loose."

Clearly, the irons were a treasure that helped this woman remember the care that her mother provided so long ago. I applaud her for letting them go when she no longer needed them, though I'm hoping that she kept the *best* iron that most strongly evoked these memories.

Hammond has turned her fascination with garage sales into a career through her Web site, GarageSaleGal.com. She offered some surprising ways to get the best return from your garage sale with the least hassle. No garage? This advice applies to yard sales, too.

Skip the price tag on your items. Traditionally, an early step in the garage sale process has been to buy a sheet of tiny stickers, write prices on them, and affix the stickers to your belongings. Don't, Hammond urges.

For one thing, those stickers cost money. They also take a lot of time to fill out. And the occasional unethical shopper may switch the price tags in order to take home an almost literal steal.

But the main reason to not price your goods is because the buyer might make a much better offer, Hammond says. "Let's say you decided you want to get rid of that 1940s sunflower-shaped cookie jar. So you'd take a dollar for it. Now, let's say someone walks up and remembers the 1940s sunflower-shaped cookie jar that they broke when they were a child. This person might easily pay $30 for this, and you've undercut yourself!"

Sell on a day when you have less competition. Put your stuff out on Friday morning and be ready to welcome early visitors, Hammond suggests. "Most people think Saturday is the best day. It's not. The best day to have a garage sale is Friday," she insists.

That's because you'll tend to draw in shoppers who are on their way to work, or who are dropping kids off at school. You'll also get more garage-sale aficionados who have fewer other sales to visit since it's a Friday.

Hammond feels that you have a greater advantage in negotiating prices compared to selling on Saturday. That's because your buyers will assume that you're in no hurry to take a low price, since you can continue the sale another day.

Advertise it well. Let as many people as possible know that you're hosting the sale. She advises against newspaper classified ads, given their cost and the shrinking audience who reads them. It's free to put your advertisement on Craigslist, but this site tends to be crowded with garage sales, she says.

If you're on social media, post the date and time of your yard sale there. Consider posting a few photos of particularly interesting pieces to help bring in shoppers. You can also easily find Web sites that run garage sale ads (including Hammond's site).

Use simple signs. Put up signs in your neighborhood that direct shoppers to your sale. (If you're hanging them from trees, telephone poles, signs, fences, and similar locations, first make sure it's okay.) Be sure to take them down after the sale!

Use fluorescent poster board to make your signs. It doesn't matter which conspicuous color you pick—pink, yellow, green, or orange—but stick with the same color for all your signs, Hammond says. This gives your shoppers an easy-to-follow trail of clues to your home. Make the signs 15 inches square—anything bigger and they'll flap in the wind and may fall off.

Finally, just put the word SALE on your sign, with an arrow pointing in the correct direction. You don't need to clutter it with your address or phone number, she says.

Pretend you're running a store. On this day, your garage is a retail environment, and you're the manager, Hammond says. Sweep the floor and provide good lighting. Have soft music playing in the background and make water, coffee, and lemonade available. (It's okay to charge for it.)

Make your merchandise look appealing, she urges. Dust it off. Group like items together, such as electronics and kitchenware. If possible, hang your clothing from racks so shoppers can browse easily.

Use a team. If possible, have at least four people working your garage sale, Hammond recommends. Having assistants helps ensure that someone is available to answer questions, negotiate prices, and take payments. You'll also want someone to go out periodically to make sure your brightly colored signs are all still up and pointing in the proper direction.

Stay safety conscious. Keep all the doors to your home locked. Keep only a small amount of money outside for making change and stow it in a fanny pack on your waist. As more money comes in from customers, periodically take it inside and stash it in a safe place.

Sometimes customers walk off with merchandise without paying. This is an unpleasant-but-not-uncommon situation at garage sales. If you see it happen, let it go, Hammond urges. Your safety is more valuable than the item.

Estate Sales: Bringing In a Professional to Bring In Shoppers

You might think of an estate sale as a bigger, more-formal version of a garage sale that's typically held in the home that you're downsizing, though sometimes an estate sale company can sell the goods in another location. The public, which may wait in line to enter the home, walks around and shops. Sometimes items are marked with a price, and sometimes shoppers place their own bids.

Estate sales aren't for every downsizer. Before deciding to host one, it's important to set realistic goals, do some advanced work, and pick an estate sale professional carefully, Hall warns. Here's how.

Figure out if an estate sale is a good fit for your needs. How much stuff do you want to sell? Some estate sale professionals will only work with you if the sale is expected to bring in at least $5,000, Hall says. Others require an even higher minimum.

Ask yourself whether buyers will be interested in the stuff you're selling. Ideally, Hall says, sellers can offer a mix of big-ticket items and unique smaller collectibles to entice a diverse crowd.

Also, is your home an ideal setting for a sale? A neighborhood association may not want hundreds of cars parked in the street during the sale. A high-rise apartment building may also frown on the foot traffic heading to a sale. On the other hand, is your home located far out in the country? People might not be willing to make the drive.

Understand what an estate sale company does. "Do not let Aunt Bessie's son's neighbor do it because he dabbles in antiques," Hall warns. A good estate sale professional must use a variety of skills in order to make your sale as successful as possible. Look for someone who can either accurately appraise your goods or call upon a network of contacts to provide this crucial service.

You'll also want someone with a proven ability to advertise your sale to the right shoppers so it brings them in like a "giant magnet," Hall says.

Do your homework on the estate professional. To find candidates who can run your estate sale, ask for references from people like your friends, your real estate agent, your lawyer, and your accountant. Interview at least three candidates before making your choice, Hall suggests.

Pay attention to these factors: Do they have a professional-looking Web site? Do they show up on time for the interview? Do they seem responsible and knowledgeable? Considering the reason why you're holding this sale, you'll probably want someone who also seems understanding and empathetic.

You can get a sense of their reputation by checking their references, the Better Business Bureau, and Angie's List, Hall says. It's also a good idea to visit a few of their sales and ask clients afterward about their experiences.

Be ready for the estate sale company to share in the profits. Expect for the company to charge 35 percent of what you bring in. You may also have to pay up-front consulting fees. When you're interviewing candidates, keep in mind that a more experienced (and expensive) company may more than make up for their fee by pricing your items more accurately and bringing in more shoppers, she says.

Consider making the sale a nonfamily event. I understand the appeal of wanting to hang around during the estate sale. It can be nice to get a sense of the people who will be providing a new home for your possessions. Maybe you'd like to tell them how much you enjoyed these items, but that can feel off-putting to estate sale buyers. The estate professional may not like having extra guests, either, Hall says. That's because families have a tendency to disrupt the carefully planned sales environment. (She's heard of a family member telling a shopper that "Aunt Sally died in that chair!"

Sell Your Stuff Online

There's a lot to be said about turning to the Internet to unload your extra stuff. For starters, you can connect with three billion potential shoppers around the world. You also have access to popular sites that make it relatively easy to reach these people— like Amazon, Craigslist, and eBay—and many lesser-known sites to help you sell specific items like electronics and clothes.

Note that I said *relatively* easy. Selling your stuff online can still be challenging, especially if you're in a hurry to move.

You're competing with a lot of other sellers, so you'll need to have interesting stuff, and you'll need to cleverly market it at a good price. You also must know the ins and outs of how these sites work, and you'll need to know how to interact safely with the spectrum of unique people you'll encounter online, including scammers.

Each site has its own rules and customs. I'd recommend that you do some research online for the sites that best meet your needs (for example, how much will you have to pay the site? How convenient is it to use? Will you need to meet the buyer in person or will you have to mail the items?).

Wherever you choose to sell your household items, keep these general ideas in mind.

Find the right price. Look online for the typical price that other people are setting for similar items, and list yours comparably. Also, try to get a sense of how common these things are in retail stores and on the used market.

If they're easy to obtain, that's probably going to lower your asking price. But if you suspect that you have an uncommon item, or yours seems to be in especially good condition, this is evidence that likely supports a higher asking price.

Describe the item well. When you write the title and description for the item, use keywords that will bring up the listing when shoppers search for it. If they can't find it, they can't buy it! If you were looking for this thing, what words would *you* put in the search box?

Also, use lively writing to make the item sound appealing (think like an advertiser or marketer would), but accurately describe the item. If it has damaged spots or flaws, acknowledge them, too. Finally, use good grammar and spelling. This gives you the air of a well-informed seller, and it makes your wares more attractive.

Take great pictures. The photo you include of your item can make shoppers reach for their credit cards or run the other way. So take time to make it good. Be sure the item is clean and free of dust. If possible, shoot the photo in natural light (in other words, sunlight) and place the object against a noncluttered, plain background.

Be sure that you're close enough to capture details of the object that will interest the buyer. If it's large, you might want to post a close-up or two alongside a photo of the entire thing.

Respond to user questions. When you walk into a retail store and can't find any employees to answer your questions, how likely are you to make a purchase? The same is true when you offer items for sale online. Your potential buyers are probably going to want to ask for more details about your item. So regularly check for messages so you can answer these questions promptly.

STEP 8: DONATE REMAINING ITEMS

Give away your remaining:

Trinkets	I-Might-Need-It Items that
Forgotten items	you didn't find worthy of keeping

You're very close to being finished with your downsizing. If you have items with value that you couldn't sell in a garage sale, estate sale, or online—or you decided not to bother trying to sell them—it's time to donate them to charity.

Just like *you* pass through stages in your life, so does your stuff. But in today's disposable culture, too many of our items don't get to reach their later stages. They're new and trendy, slightly used, worn and obsolete, then too often they go into a landfill (or the back of a cabinet or closet for a few years, then the landfill). It's often easier to throw them away than make a few phone calls or drive a few miles to find someone who wants them.

You brought these items into your home because you saw some type of value in them. I set up the *Let It Go* process to help you extract as much of that value from your possessions as possible.

Your remaining I-Might-Need-It Items can provide a fun moment for a kid who wouldn't otherwise have it, clothes for an unemployed person who wants to make a good impression at a job interview, appliances to parents starting over after a crisis, or just a bit of joy to people who love bargains. Your items also support jobs for the people who process and handle them.

In return, you may be able to deduct the value of the goods you donate at tax time. When possible, get a receipt from the organization, listing the date of the donation and the items you gave. Talk to your tax professional—or check out the IRS Web site—to learn more about how this process works.

You can also learn more about groups in your area that accept household items at CharityNavigator.org.

As you select items to donate, ask yourself: *"Would I feel good about giving this toy to my child in its present state? Would I feel good about my guests sitting on this couch? Does this blender have a lid, and does it turn on when I plug it in?"* If the answer is no, then don't pass it along to the charitable organization. The more trash they have to sort out, the more work they must pay someone to do.

That said, some will sell overly worn or stained clothing to recyclers. If you're uncertain whether your items will be useful, call and ask! Also, if the organization sends out a truck to pick up your goods, make sure to set them out on time so the hauler doesn't waste a trip.

STEP 9: DISPOSE OF TRASH

Throw away or recycle your remaining:

Trinkets   Malignant items

Forgotten items   Household trash

I-Might-Need-It Items
    that you didn't find
    worthy of keeping

Congratulations—you've reached the end of your downsizing! But even at the finish line, you still have a bit of important work to do to ensure that your downsizing is as meaningful and sustainable as it can be.

To the extent that your community makes it possible, please recycle as much of your trash as you can. Take hazardous items (like household chemicals, old batteries, cans of paint) to the approved drop-off site in your area, or ask your trash service about options it can offer for these items.

Also, make use of the many options you have to recycle your unwanted electronic devices. Again, your community may offer a drop-off point for these items. Some big-box electronics and office-supply stores will also accept these devices and some other household appliances. For recycling sites available in your area, check out GreenerGadgets.org.

Just make sure that the organization you plan to use will accept the specific items you want to recycle. (In some cases, you may have to pay a fee.) Also, even if the organization says it will wipe the data off your old computer, tablet, or other device, it's wise to do this yourself before you drop it off.

Hopefully, after you've repeatedly sifted through your household's "material convoy" with each of these steps, all you're left with is stuff that really, truly has nowhere else to go but the landfill.

Bag it up and set it out in the appropriate place for your trash collector to take it.

You can now consider your home thoroughly and completely downsized in the *Let It Go* manner. I would send you a certificate of completion, but that would just be clutter you don't need, wouldn't it?

Now, stow this book somewhere you can find it when you get to your next destination. Once you're unpacked and settled in, please find a quiet moment and go to the Afterword on page 231.

THE **LET IT GO** FLOWCHART FOR DOWNSIZING YOUR OWN HOME

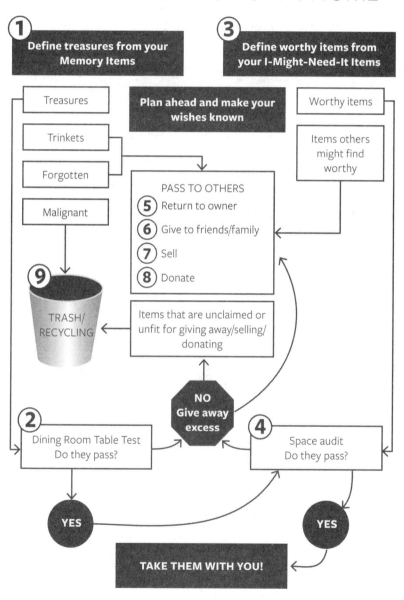

CHAPTER 8

Downsizing Your Parents' Home

Some of the biggest and most familiar brands in the United States are family endeavors. Go behind the scenes at Ford, Walmart, and Gap, and you'll see the founders' children, grandchildren, or even great-grandchildren helping to run the company.

That said, it's common for families to lose their businesses fairly quickly. According to *Harvard Business Review*, nearly three in four family-owned businesses either fail or land in outsiders' hands before the second generation is able to take over.

As I mentioned in Chapter 5, if your downsizing project involves family members, which they typically do, then you should approach it as you would a family business.

So it's reasonable to ask why, if so many family businesses fall apart, I would want you to run your downsizing like one. Because you can learn what *not* to do from them.

These businesses sometimes implode from problems similar to those that can arise when you're downsizing: Family members feud. They form factions. They let their emotions spill over into their decisions. They get resentful.

But when they plan carefully and follow a few sensible rules, family businesses can thrive. Success can also be yours in the downsizing "business" so long as you organize it thoughtfully and run it the right way.

In this chapter, I'm going to guide you through the process of downsizing your parents' home. Different situations can press you into this service, but I suspect these typically fall into two categories:

- One or both parents need to move into an assisted living facility or nursing home
- One or both parents have passed away

If your parents are facing a health emergency that demands speed and quick decisions, this downsizing may be sudden. Or you may have the luxury of time before you need to dive into the process.

In all cases, however, the outcome you want is the same: for you and your family members to be happy, for your parents' wishes to be honored, and for the process to be as efficient as possible.

DOWNSIZING WHEN A PARENT IS MOVING TO LONG-TERM CARE

Your downsizing project may arise when mom, dad, or both need to move out of their home because dementia or another health issue prevents them from living independently.

They may go to a nursing home, assisted living facility, or even a family member's home. Though these are different kinds of living arrangements, for the sake of convenience, I'll refer to them as long-term care. I anticipate that in these situations you'll have a high degree of input because their participation may be more limited.

If mom and dad are downsizing to an active retirement community under their own steam, you'll find plenty of material in this chapter that will apply to your situation, but your parents will have much more say in directing the process.

Depending on their needs, your parents may be downsizing their possessions and letting their home go now, perhaps to free up money for their care or to reduce expenses on mortgage, rent, or utilities on an empty house. Or they may decide to keep the home for now. Perhaps someone is still living there, or they hope to return home from their residential arrangement someday.

Either way, you'll need to sort through your parents' belongings to some degree—if not their entire home, then just to pick out some possessions that create a sense of home in their new living space.

STEP 1: PROVIDE A FAMILIAR ATMOSPHERE FOR A PARENT'S NEW HOME

Moving to long-term care is a monumental step for seniors and their families. Odds are good it will be your parents' final home. Though it comes with benefits—like improved safety and security and less responsibility—the move also brings changes that can cause distress.

Mom and dad may feel like they're losing independence, their lives are shrinking dramatically, or their mental or physical health is declining. In addition to the sadness or even grief over this move, they may be anxious about the cost of their care.

For families, the move often triggers a huge amount of guilt. Adult children may feel that they're abandoning the people who spent a lifetime nurturing and caring for them. Also, your parents may be yielding some degree of decision-making power to you, but you aren't yet comfortable with your new role.

If your parent is moving into one of your homes, the sibling who is becoming the main caregiver will have major new responsibilities. None of this is easy, and emotions often run high.

However, moving a parent to assisted living can bear several

Real-World Downsizing Discovery

Terri says: When my mother passed away, she left a beautiful home filled with lovely furniture, art, and collectibles. She also had china and glassware from my grandmother. I didn't know what I was supposed to do with all of it, since I had my own home filled with my own furniture and personal pieces. The loss of my mom was hard enough, but I didn't want to disrespect her memory.

My aunt told me something that helped me through it, and I have shared it with everyone I know who has gone through the same situation: "These things served the purpose of making your mom happy. She loved them. Their purpose is not to make *you* happy. Their purpose is done." I can't tell you how that one conversation changed my life!

gifts for you. For one thing, it provides a simple, lower-pressure way to introduce your family to the downsizing process. Also, though you don't have to *love* the changes that are happening to your parent, learning to view them as a natural part of everyone's journey can help to lessen your pain. Applying this new point of view to your own aging process may help you accept it more easily in coming years.

A third gift is this: As you move your parent, along with his or her most important possessions, you'll see how your fellow participants handle the tasks involved in the move. You'll also start practicing how to work together before your bigger parent-related downsizing project—following the death of your parent—down the road.

Keep the following steps in mind to help a parent create an environment that's comforting and familiar.

Provide as much decision-making power as possible. Big changes in our lives often feel scary. But the degree of control we have over them can work like a volume knob to turn down our fear.

Be sure that your parent provides as much input as possible on the furnishings, decorations, personal treasures, and other items that will outfit the new living space. If mom or dad cannot communicate due to dementia or other health problems, you'll have to use your best judgment to make these decisions.

A note here: Your parents may resist the idea of bringing objects from home. Resistance usually signals something deeper going on, so dig down to find the real source of distress. It may be that dad doesn't like the idea of needing long-term care, and he's telling himself that he'll return home someday, so there's no reason to move his stuff. Be patient and follow his lead.

Consider the size of the apartment or room. Moving to a care facility requires a drastic downsizing. Your loved one's space for living and storage tends to be quite limited and unyielding, so it's usually impossible to take a large number of household items or pieces of furniture.

When you settle on a facility, measure the space that will belong to your parent. Even better, ask for a blueprint of the area from the management.

This is how much room you'll have to work with. Avoid trying to cram as much as you can within this space. You'll want to reduce clutter and other obstacles, such as rugs, that can cause your parent to fall. You'll also need to provide open space so nursing staff and other assistants can move freely.

If your parent is sharing a space in a facility with a roommate, be sure that the stuff you bring from home doesn't encroach on the other resident or the resident's family.

Walk through the facility and observe how other rooms are outfitted (without violating anyone's privacy). Ask the management if they have a list of suggestions for the type of household goods that residents typically need.

MOM IS IN THE NURSING HOME— DOES SHE STILL NEED HER STUFF?

If one or both of your parents are in a long-term care facility and can no longer make decisions, can you sell their home and divide up their possessions now?

Maybe. But it's critical that you speak with your parents' estate attorney, follow their wishes, and understand the possible financial implications.

For starters, someone needs a durable power of attorney who provides the ability to make this decision for your parent, says Larry Lehmann, an estate planning attorney in New Orleans and the president of the National Association of Estate Planners and Councils. This is a legal document that allows a representative—such as an adult child or trusted friend—to make certain types of decisions on your parents' behalf when they can't.

Second, the person with the durable power of attorney needs to make decisions that are in your parents' best interest. Would you be selling the home or dividing up the stuff because *you* want it, or because mom would want it done? Selling the home doesn't appear to be the right move "if you know mom would be devastated if you sold the house, and there are other resources" to pay for her care, Lehmann says.

Taking certain actions while a parent is in long-term care may come at a large cost. For example, if Medicaid is covering your parents' nursing home bill, their house may be exempt from being sold while they're alive to reimburse the state for their care, Lehmann says. But if you sell their home, the state may be able to recoup its expenses on their care from the proceeds of the sale. If they transfer the home into someone else's name, they may become ineligible for Medicaid.

Talk to a qualified legal and accounting professional—I'm neither of these!—before taking these types of actions.

Ask about the facility's rules. While you're getting the specifications of the room, ask the management about any rules that will limit the types of belongings your parent can bring. Can you hang framed paintings or photos on the wall? Can you keep potted plants in the room? Can you bring your own furniture, or is it provided?

Supply familiar and functional items. Focus on providing two types of belongings: treasures (the possessions that recall mom's best moments, most important memories, or greatest achievements) and worthy items (useful objects that support familiar comforts and instill a sense of home).

Think about the kind of treasures *you* would want if you had to re-create your life in a much smaller setting. What are your most valued memories? What components of your identity have always been most important to you? Now help mom do this exercise.

What items does she use from day to day, like her reading glasses, puzzle books, craft supplies, and favorite clothing and shoes? These will also help her stay as mentally and physically engaged as possible.

These special items from your parent's life will help to create a sense of calm. Choose them carefully and arrange them well in the new space.

Be practical. Outfit the room from your *parent's* perspective. Can dad still easily get up from the upholstered chair you were planning to bring? If not, a lift chair may be a wise investment. If mom has poor vision or spends most of her time lying down, make sure you don't put family photos somewhere she can't see them, like on top of a high cabinet.

STEP 2: BE SURE YOUR PARENTS' LEGAL PAPERWORK IS IN ORDER

Several legal documents allow parents to express their wishes about important matters ahead of time. These documents can eliminate confusion and prevent a lot of turmoil among family members after mom and dad are gone.

Hopefully, your parents took these steps—on their own or, more likely, with the help of an attorney—long before they needed some type of assisted living. If they did, it's a good idea for at least one family member to know where these documents are and what they specify.

If they haven't created legally valid versions of the following documents (and rechecked them recently to ensure they're still accurate), I recommend that you and they consult an experienced attorney to look into doing so now.

- **A will and/or a living trust.** These specify how your parents want their property distributed after their death. Depending on their specific needs, they may want a will, a trust, or

"WHITE LIES" FOR THE RIGHT REASONS CAN HAVE A PLACE IN DOWNSIZING

Okay, I know I say that openness, honesty, and transparency are crucial during downsizing. But sometimes it's appropriate to not tell the entire truth.

For example, your mother demands that you take Aunt Annie's umbrella stand, but you have absolutely no use—or space—for it. You have let your mother know this, but she keeps pushing it on you.

You're not obligated to take or keep any item. If a loved one is trying to guilt you into taking an object, that's even *more* of a reason not to accept it. In this case, it's appropriate to say, "Why, yes, I'd love to take that thing, after all," without mentioning, "I'd love to take it to the Salvation Army, which is where I'm stopping on the way home."

both. Each has unique characteristics, advantages, and disadvantages that an estate attorney can describe to you.

- **A living will.** Among other things, this specifies what kind of medical treatment your parents want at the end of their lives. At some point, do you ask the doctors to step back and just keep your parent comfortable until the end? Or does your parent want every treatment the doctors can provide in order to stay alive as long as possible? This document lets your parents decide . . . so you don't have to.

- **Durable power of attorney.** This allows a trusted adult—perhaps you or one of your siblings—to step in and make decisions on behalf of your parents if they become incapacitated. It's possible to give one person the power to handle different types of health-care and financial decisions. Or

If your mother asks you if she will ever be able to move back home from long-term care, but you and her doctor just don't think it's possible, ideally you'll be able to explain the situation honestly to her. But in some cases, such as when dementia is a factor, it may be okay to say, "Possibly! Let's just keep an eye on things."

Sometimes a white lie might be appropriate with your kids, too. As Lysa, a Facebook follower, shared with me: "We're doing a big move, so we're culling ruthlessly! We've been carting our daughter's ballet costumes, trophies, books and assignments, and large boxes of her things, and as we've been downsizing, I'd text her and say, 'Oh no, a mouse must have gotten in with your papers and school assignments.' Her instant reply—since she lives in another state—was, 'Get rid of them! Yuck, throw them out!!!' I wish I'd thought of it years ago. I hope she doesn't read this . . . there never was a mouse!"

your parent can give one person power of attorney for health-care matters and someone else power of attorney for money-related issues.

STEP 3: CONSIDER DISTRIBUTING SOME ITEMS IN ADVANCE

If your parents want to give particular items to family members while they're alive, now may be a good time to do so. (Discuss any handovers with your parents' estate attorney to make sure that they don't lead to any surprise legal or financial consequences.)

Or you may want to work with your siblings now (or others who will inherit from your parents) to start calling dibs on particular items that aren't covered in the will or trust. With your parents' permission, use family holiday dinners and other gatherings to start claiming items in advance. If everyone is in agreement, perhaps the person claiming an object can put a little sticker on it (like on the back of a picture frame or under the base of a lamp), or everyone can log their choices in a book.

If everyone can get started in a relaxed, happy frame of mind while one or both parents are alive, it can help your family reduce the need for decisions later under the shadow of stress and grief.

DOWNSIZING YOUR PARENTS' BELONGINGS WHEN THEY'RE GONE

STEP 4: LOOK TO YOUR PARENTS' WISHES

This book is aimed at helping you make the best decisions about physical possessions that you own, or will own when you inherit them. After your parents pass away, legal documents and proceedings will likely determine how at least part of their estate is distributed. I'm not a legal expert, and the purpose of this book isn't to advise you how to divide up any bank accounts, retirement nest eggs, real estate, or life insurance that your parents left.

But I can say that the first step in downsizing after your parents are gone is to comply with the many legal requirements that arise. It's important to also listen to your parents' wishes on who should receive what. They may have gone into great detail about how their household possessions should be divided. Or they may give you and their other heirs more freedom to divide up their estate in a fair manner as you see fit.

So now is the time to follow the wishes that your parents expressed. Unfortunately, now is also the time when your family may resist discussing how the estate will be divided. Or some families start bickering and voicing their displeasure with the will or other legal directions very early. I would urge you to create an atmosphere of understanding and collaboration from the very beginning. Try to start working as a team as soon as you can.

If your parents created a will, that will typically has an *executor*, notes Brian Caverly, a semi-retired Pennsylvania attorney and author of *Estate Planning for Dummies*. This is the person who's legally charged with ensuring that everyone follows the directions in the will. This includes dividing up your parents' estate like they wanted and making sure that the estate pays any bills or debts that your parents still owed. If your parents created a trust, it will have a *trustee*, who has a similar responsibility to carry out your parents' wishes.

Your parents may have chosen you or one of your siblings to take on the role of executor or trustee. Or perhaps several siblings are declared coexecutors or co-trustees. However, sometimes people look to outsiders to take this role, such as a lawyer or family friend.

These roles are an important responsibility. Hopefully, your parents put careful thought into picking the person to take this job. The executor or trustee speaks for your parents now that they can no longer do so, and distributes the assets that they worked so hard to attain. It's a big job that can be stressful and quite time-consuming.

If you're the executor or trustee, understand that a lot of people are counting on you to do this job well. You're likely going to have to file tax returns, keep track of the value of your parents' assets, and manage a lot of details during a time when you're probably not feeling your strongest emotionally. You may also have to defend your late parents' wishes to unhappy family members. Understand your duties and know what you can and cannot do in this role. Be ready to reach out for assistance from a lawyer or accountant if you're unclear about any task.

Also, keep careful records and be completely transparent with your siblings and any other heirs. Avoid giving them any reason to be suspicious of how you're handling money or property. If they do question any of your actions, be ready to show documentation for everything you've done.

If a sibling is the executor or trustee, understand that this person may feel an extra degree of pressure during the downsizing. Be ready to provide help as needed. Also understand that this person is likely entitled by law to take compensation from the estate for doing this job. He or she may accept it (which is a reasonable choice, given the work involved) or choose to turn it down (perhaps to preserve family unity).

If someone outside the family is the executor or trustee, it's a good idea to double-check to ensure that this person is meeting all the deadlines, handling the tasks appropriately, and following the directions of the legal document your parents created.

STEP 5: CREATE AN INFORMAL DOWNSIZING BUSINESS

I'm assuming that at this point, your family has followed your parents' will or other legal documents that directed where any specific belongings should go. The rest of the steps now deal with the remaining possessions that are available for you to divide with your parents' other heirs.

You'll have two types of belongings to distribute:

- "Treasures," which are the irreplaceable items that recall memories of your family's "bests, mosts, and greatests."

- "Worthy" possessions that have more practical or monetary value than sentimental value. These are the power tools, sewing machines, furniture, clothes, and other useful objects in the "material convoy" that trailed behind your parents during their lives.

To keep it simple, I'm going to use the term "siblings" from now on to mean "everyone who gets a portion of your parents' belongings." But it's possible that your parents have left one or more of your siblings out of the will or declared that some other person should also receive items, such as one of your aunts, uncles, or cousins, or even a nonfamily member.

So the rest of the downsizing process may only involve you and your siblings. But include anyone else who should play a role, as your parents requested.

Your next task is to create a type of "family business" devoted to downsizing. This business doesn't have its own

office. It doesn't require you to suspend your family relationships. But it does entail using a deliberate, well-organized, and
professional approach for the task at hand.

You and your siblings have an important job that needs
to be done efficiently and effectively, without excessive emotion derailing the process (in other words, in a businesslike
manner!).

Without some type of formalized structure for your downsizing, the process can turn into a free-for-all that leads to hurt
feelings, resentment, financial losses, and missing treasures.
*"What do you mean you just threw it away? Who said you
could keep this? That's not fair, and if Mom were here, I know
she'd tell you so!"*

Sticking to the following rules will help your family sail
through this event on calm and peaceful waters.

1. Decide on stakeholders. Define exactly who gets to play a
role in the downsizing process. Your parents' will or trust should
specify who gets a cut of your parents' estate, but it likely won't
list who will receive every single item in the home, or who
should come together to help clear out the house.

Determine whether siblings' spouses will have a say in these
decisions. I can envision scenarios where this would work just
fine. But in many cases, like large families that already have a
lot of participants or families in which brothers- and sisters-in-
law are kept a little distant from family decisions, giving spouses
a vote on the downsizing might create dissent.

This is your group's call, but I would suggest *not* giving
spouses decision-making power. Doing so adds handfuls of
extra pieces to the puzzle you're trying to solve.

It may be difficult for you to insist that the decisions only
involve blood relatives, but this request may prevent later conflict. Decide what's best for the downsizing project, not

what's easiest in the face of strong personalities and emotional sensitivities.

2. Hold a first meeting. This meeting will determine the tone of the whole downsizing process. Begin by setting a reasonable time and place for the first meeting so everyone can attend (or participate remotely by phone or Skype if they can't join in person). Have a clear agenda and make sure that everyone has a say in the proceedings. Start agreeing upon outcomes you want to achieve from the downsizing, the action steps that the downsizing will require, and the language that's to be used whenever conflict might arise. Remember: Treat this as you would a business.

3. Set up ground rules and timelines. Siblings can use different options for dividing treasures (I'll provide them later in this chapter) and turning worthy items with value into cash (also in this chapter). Decide on the strategies that you're going to use in the downsizing process.

For example, do you want to sell everything that the siblings don't want to keep, even though this requires more work? Or do you want to donate all the belongings of value, which is easier and more altruistic, but potentially less lucrative? (You won't get cash up front, though you may reap tax benefits later.)

Also agree on a timeline. Make sure everyone knows when the downsizing should be completed. All the participants also need to know when other actions should be taken, such as when a garage sale or estate sale should be held, and when the house will be put on the market.

Your group may not be able to create a firm timeline for all these targets immediately. But as plans come together, share the details with everyone who needs to know.

4. Assign jobs. Downsizing involves a lot of skill sets. You have logistics to plan, packing supplies to buy, numbers to add up, calls to make, bills to pay, and forms to sign. One or more strong backs are also very helpful, if not mandatory.

Figure out who is going to help and what they'll be doing. I think it's reasonable to expect assistance from anyone who's going to be keeping items or benefiting from this downsizing. If any participating family members are out of state, try to find a way for them to pitch in their fair share, whether they come in for a long weekend visit to help in person, make phone calls to line up professionals, or manage logistics from afar. It's also reasonable for people to help out according to their skills and interests.

Also, if a sibling is an executor or trustee, you may want to take these responsibilities into account when dividing tasks fairly.

Keep in mind that families often distribute downsizing chores along gender lines. If women want to clean the kitchen and organize family photos and men want to carry boxes, that's fine. But discuss it first and don't presume that women and men will naturally volunteer for certain jobs. (See page 106.)

5. Expect transparency. You're going to need a lot of honesty from your fellow participants. This means that everyone must talk openly about what they want.

Everyone involved will bring all sorts of strongly held values to the table. These values will influence which of the home's possessions they want to keep, throw away, or sell.

For example, your parents' possessions will represent different possibilities for family members. Some may want to preserve their history, some may want to bring home free household goods, and others may see a chance to sell items to improve their finances. All of these motivations, within reason, may be appropriate desires. Sometimes participants' values will clash. Sometimes your family members may not be able to describe their values because they're so deeply buried.

So try to draw them out. If people feel strongly about a particular decision that's contributing to a conflict, encourage them to explain *why*. Even if their stance is unpopular or divisive at first, the rest of the group may feel differently if they hear the explanation.

Transparency also means that participants can't hide their actions from the others. Nor can they say one thing and do something else. Ideally, each person will alert the others before doing anything major (like taking an item that everyone wants, hiring outside help such as an estate sale company, or making important decisions).

That said, it's okay to take some actions and make minor decisions without distracting everyone with calls and e-mails. But as much as possible, each participant needs to work with openness and honesty.

6. Communicate! This goes hand-in-hand with transparency. Communicate early and often. Participants cannot make decisions for someone else without discussing them first, just because they're "certain" they know what this person would want.

So be sure you have contact information (including cell phone numbers and e-mail addresses) for everyone involved.

If a lot of people are participating in the process, especially if you're separated by distance, you may want to set up an online meeting place to leave notes and update a calendar. You can find family organizer apps, and Google Drive allows multiple people to access shared documents.

7. Hold regular meetings. After your first meeting, bring your decision makers together to exchange ideas and conduct the downsizing process, as needed. How many meetings you'll need depends on the size of your family, the amount of property you'll be going through, how well the participants get along,

ACTION STEPS IMPORTANT
IN FAMILY DOWNSIZING

Action steps are things that participants at the meeting agree
will take place either before the next meeting or within a certain amount of time. Be sure to write down all the agreed-upon
action steps and who is responsible for completing them. A
review of the previous action steps should be the first item on
the agenda of any meeting.

and where you're spread out geographically. If it's just you and
one sibling who lives nearby, the first planning meeting may
suffice.

Each meeting needs to have goals, and it needs to lead to
action steps for members to follow afterward. Hold everyone
responsible for sticking to the meeting's agenda. If one of the
downsizing disrupters from Chapter 5 wants to hijack the
meeting (likely the Control Freak, the Provocateur, or the
Attention Seeker), politely tell this person that you want to
hear what he or she has to say, but it's either going to have to
wait until the scheduled business is handled, or it will require
a new meeting.

Although emotions may run high during the downsizing, and
separating your feelings from your family possessions can be
difficult, it's important for participants not to act and react from
a highly emotional place during these discussions. It's unlikely
that you'd shout or cry during a staff meeting or a business function. Similarly, this behavior shouldn't have a place at these
downsizing meetings.

8. Compromise, but be ready to let it go. When conflicts
arise, try to settle them as soon as possible. At some point, you

or another participant will probably lose a treasure that you hoped to keep, or you'll fail to get your way on an important decision.

If someone else gets a treasure you wanted, can you find a partially acceptable solution? Would you be satisfied with taking a picture of this painting or vase? Can you trade it back and forth periodically? Can you find a different treasure in your parents' home that evokes a similar memory?

If none of these compromises work, just remember that letting go during downsizing sometimes means you have to let go of disappointment and resentment over decisions that didn't end like you wanted. It's not likely that everyone will be 100 percent happy with every decision. That's just the way these situations work out.

STEP 6: DIVIDE YOUR FAMILY'S TREASURES

As you stand in your parents' home and prepare to distribute their stuff, I recommend that everyone start by asking for the treasures that are deeply important to them. Generally speaking, these are the things you want to keep because they have a high *sentimental* value, not because you can resell them for their *monetary* value. You'll likely keep these in a safe place for the rest of your life, then offer them to your own kids.

These treasures are the best type of Memory Item you'll find in your parents' house. As you may recall from page 84, the other types of objects in this category are:

The trinkets   The malignant

The forgotten

As much as possible, take home only treasures, not these other types of memory-related possessions. If a trinket or long-forgotten item rises to the level of a treasure, then keep it. If not, let it go. Throw away any malignant items you find in your parents' home. These are the objects that raise negative or painful memories or emotions.

Earlier in the book, I described the treasure map exercise that helps you find the treasures within your own household collection, and it will also work well as you downsize your parents' possessions. (It's on page 93.) To create a treasure map for your parents' home, start by coming up with your most important memories of your parents, your grandparents, and your childhood that you want to preserve. These are the "bests, mosts, and greatests" of your past, like:

- The best artwork I created as a child

- The greatest vacation we took when I was growing up

- My favorite memory of the times I spent with my grandmother (and grandfather, favorite aunt, and so forth)

- The best example of mom or dad's creativity

How many items you choose is up to you. If your parents' estate is small, or they didn't keep many sentimental items, or you have six siblings like I do, you might only come away with a few treasures.

But if their home was large and full of goodies, you should still put a limit on yourself. I recommend the Dining Room Table Test here: Take no more than the number of objects that will fit on the dining room table in your home. Also, try to come up with your "bests, mosts, and greatests" memory list *first*, then find objects tied to those memories, rather than picking items and then coming up with a rationale for why you should keep them.

I recommend that you share this treasure-finding strategy

with your siblings. I hope that they will see the value in following it, as this will probably help you work better as a team. But they're free to ask for the items they want, as long as their requests are fair to everyone. As far as you are concerned, only take items that you truly feel are treasures, instead of trying to get as many objects as your siblings are claiming. Only worry about what's important to *you*.

Downsizing your parents' stuff is not about achieving an equal score. It's about carrying away the take-home message you need to hear from your parents. Within my own family, we were fascinated to hear what our siblings wanted. Everyone was captivated by the stories of what a sibling remembered about a moment or an object. Interestingly, almost none of the treasures that my brother and sisters and I identified had any real monetary value.

Inevitably, two or more people in your family will want to claim the same treasure. So I recommend that everyone first make up his or her own treasure map, then participate in an agreed-upon method that helps ensure that all have an equal chance to take home as much of their list as possible.

You can deploy the following options as they're written here, adjust the details for your family's individual needs, or even use them in combination.

1. Get back what you gave. Here's an easy way to start distributing mom and dad's possessions. Whoever *gave* them an item gets the first opportunity to *take* it. This is how my siblings and I began the process of downsizing our mother's house.

I suspect that your emotional attachment to objects you gave your parents may not be especially strong, and these items probably won't comprise a major portion of your treasure map. Still, it will get your process started. Plus, figuring out who gave your parents which item is generally easy to determine, so it's not likely to spawn arguments. You want to start your downsizing effort with a success, and this step should provide it.

2. Go back to the request list you made in advance. Was your family able to act on Step 3 of this process (see page 200) while one or both parents were alive? This is the step in which your parent suggests where particular items should go, and you and your siblings announce your wishes for items.

If so, start collecting the possessions that mom or dad wanted you to have or that you requested back then.

3. Let chance have its say. Ask all the participants to draw straws, roll dice, or pick a number to determine the order in which people get to choose the treasure they want. (*Don't* go by age or height!) Whoever goes first gets to walk through the home and pick one treasure.

Then the second person goes, followed by the third, and so on. Once everyone has had a turn, then the participants draw numbers or roll the dice again and choose another treasure. As people get their fill of the items they want, they can drop out. Once everyone is satisfied, the group can then turn its attention to the next category of possessions in the home: the worthy items that have some functional or monetary value.

A warning here: Though treasures are intended to be primarily *sentimental* items, some of these things will also have mone-

UNCOVER FAMILY STORIES
WHILE DOWNSIZING

I encourage you to share stories about the objects that are important or special to you. You'll be amazed at the insights you'll gain into your family members. No one's memories are the same, and a moment or object that seems insignificant to you may have been life-changing for someone else. The opportunity to learn about those close to you is a major gift from this downsizing experience.

START HELPING *YOUR* KIDS WITH THEIR FUTURE PARENT DOWNSIZING

Never waste an opportunity to do some advance downsizing of your own! As you go through your parents' home, apply what you're learning to your own possessions.

Do you have a treasure that you would like a specific child, grandchild, niece, or nephew to keep? Do you have a family heirloom that you would like to be donated to a local museum? Now's the time to put your wish in writing and discuss it with your family.

Or do you not care too much about what happens to your stuff after you're gone? Let your heirs know this, too. By discussing your wishes, you may help reduce squabbles after you're gone. You can also prevent your kids from feeling guilty that they don't know what to do with your stuff.

tary value. You may want to exclude certain expensive items, like gold coins or vehicles, before starting this method. Your group may also want to set a maximum value of the treasures that each person may take free of charge. If someone chooses a pile of sentimental treasures that are worth more than, say, $500, perhaps the excess will be deducted from his or her share of the proceeds of the rest of the estate.

STEP 7: DISTRIBUTE THE "WORTHY" ITEMS

At this point, you and your siblings have claimed all the sentimental treasures and family heirlooms you wanted from your parents' home. The items that remain are what I call the I-Might-Need-It Items. These fall into two categories.

Worthy items that you want. These are functional items that you would use regularly *right now* if you had them, and you have a reasonable amount of space in your home for them. Do you like to gaze at the planets and stars with your kids when you're camping? Then mom's telescope sounds like a worthy item. Do you think maybe you'd like to use her telescope someday after you move to the countryside, and you'll put it under your bed for now? Then it's not a worthy item.

Is your coffeemaker ready to be retired? Take home dad's almost-new one, and you can remember him each time you make a cup. Is your daughter a freshly graduated art student

AVOID THE COMMON "WORTHY" ERRORS

I have worked with many families whose grief, procrastination, or lack of planning has led them to keep everything of value they can from the family home.

In some cases, they emptied their wallets to ship huge piles of stuff across the country or pay for long-term storage units. Or they filled their garages and homes with stuff that was neither worthy items nor treasures. It was just an overflowing shrine to their parents made up of clutter.

Just because a worthy item is free, or your parents once used it, doesn't mean it deserves a place in *your* home. Keep these suggestions in mind.

One in, one out. If you bring a dish from your parents' home into your home because it's a worthy item, you have to get rid of a dish that's currently in your cabinet. The same is true for clothing, fishing rods, or hedge clippers. When you bring home worthy items from your parents' house, it's to *replace* something that you no longer want, or it's to gain a useful item that you don't already have. Effective downsizing does not create duplicate items!

struggling to set up her first apartment? Perhaps she can do something creative with a few items of furniture.

Just as with the treasures, you have many options for how to divide the worthy items. Perhaps you roll the dice or draw numbers out of a hat again, then take turns picking up items that you could use. Just remember, you'll need to account for the value of the items that each person takes. Does everyone get a limit? Do you set the value of the items based on their original price, or what they'd cost today? Establish your rules ahead of time.

However, this does not apply to the *treasures* you bring home, since you're keeping them for sentimental reasons, not because they perform a useful function.

You have to use it now. Are you tempted to haul in dad's like-new sump pump because the old model chugging away in your basement will probably wear out in a few years? Want to stash a nice rug away in your closet because your daughter is searching for a home with lots of hardwood floors?

Nope. That's against the *Let It Go* rules. Items are worthy because they're useful *right now.* If you don't have a specific plan to use them now—or at most in the next few months—then they're not really useful, are they?

The item must go into a living area of your home. Will you be placing the worthy item you're eyeing in your kitchen, living room, bedroom, or bathroom? That's a good sign that it's actually worthy. Will you be sticking it in your basement, garage, or attic? Then it likely fails the "Is this worthy?" test.

Worthy items that others could use. These are functional items that would still have value for someone else, just not you. If your siblings don't want them, someone else will.

Once everyone has spoken for the worthy items they want, consider allowing other people who knew your parents to pick out keepsakes that *they* would use regularly (or regard as treasures, for that matter). The list might include aunts, uncles, cousins, and your parents' friends, neighbors, and fellow worship congregants.

Though your parents are gone, they'll continue to live on in the memories and stories that these people carry around. I think this is a great way to extend your parents' legacy.

Of course, you and your siblings have the option of bundling up all the worthy items right away and selling them for cash or donating them for tax purposes, instead of distributing them to yourselves and friends and distant family. Or you can go this route with the remaining items after everyone takes home what they want.

Real-World Downsizing Discovery

Ellen says: After our mother's death, my only brother and I had the arduous task of digging through all the papers and memories she kept throughout the years. As I held 12 years' worth of my report cards and went to put them in the "keep" pile, he grabbed them, looked me in the eye, and asked "Why?" When it came to his stuff, I did the same. Though sad, the task brought us so much closer as we shared the memories and stories with just each other. I will treasure it forever! In my own house, I am constantly going through papers, since I never want my son to have to do that chore alone!

STEP 8: OFFER WORTHWHILE ITEMS FOR SALE THAT YOU AND YOUR SIBLINGS DON'T WANT

After distributing the treasures and worthy items throughout your family (and perhaps to people who cared about your parents), you and your siblings have several options if you want to sell the items of value that remain. Choices include a garage sale, an estate sale, or selling the items online. I'd like to offer some suggestions on how to use these strategies efficiently.

Not only can these steps turn your parents' valuables into money that becomes part of their legacy, they also offer a way for you to share your parents' stories. (You could include a note-card with each item you sell that tells a little anecdote of how your parent used or cared about the item.)

Before we discuss these options in depth, I'd like to help you develop some realistic expectations about the money you might make. If your parents were wealthy collectors of art and antiques, then you may enjoy a windfall when you sell their possessions. Even if your parents had more modest circumstances, maybe you'll be lucky enough to have one of those *Antiques Roadshow*-like stories about finding a previously unknown Norman Rockwell painting in the attic. But that's highly unlikely.

Often families find that their parents' valuables aren't so, well, *valuable*, warns Julie Hall. She's an estate sale professional and the director of the American Society of Estate Liquidators.

In Chapter 1, I discussed that few people want those huge wooden TV entertainment centers that were once common in living rooms, and many millennials don't even want a television. I was hoping to prepare you for this moment.

If buyers turn up their nose at your parents' prized possessions, the experience may feel like another painful jolt. Their reaction might feel to you like they're disrespecting your parents or criticizing their sense of style.

If this happens, in some cases your would-be buyers may simply have homes that aren't suited for what you're selling. "In the Carolinas, we have fabulous historic homes, then you see the older vintage houses from the 1930s and 1940s that are being bulldozed, either to put up a McMansion or a petite, simple midcentury look-alike. There's no dining room. There's no formal living room. It's all an open concept. This is what the thirtysomethings want," Hall says.

Or the collectibles that your mom insisted were valuable may have been at one time, but they aren't anymore. Maybe an object she had appraised years ago has fallen from favor. Maybe the silver market is down. Maybe she'd been treasuring family antiques for decades without realizing that "just because it's old doesn't mean it is valuable. They made junk in the 1850s, too," Hall says.

The price of many possessions is also being pushed downward because your potential shoppers can find objects for sale all over the world through their computers and smartphones. "I don't want to point the finger solely at huge online auctions, but when you thought something was rare in your region, go online and suddenly there's 9,432 of them on eBay," Hall says.

In addition, huge shifts in the nation's aging population mean that "thousands of our moms are dying every day. It's like a tidal wave," she says. That means a flood of household items is pouring into the market from a vast number of garages, attics, and basements at the same time.

So for all those reasons, please keep in mind that generally speaking, you don't have the upper hand in determining the value of your parents' household items. The buyers do. And "what we're seeing now is a significant decline in value and a strong buyer's market," Hall says.

As long as you go into this project with reasonable expectations, the process of selling your parents' property can be a positive experience. You'll probably make at least *some* money. You may also have the opportunity to meet the people who will be providing a new "life" for the belongings that were important to your parents. But be prepared for the time and effort involved, and decide whether that commitment is going to be worth the return you'll likely have.

Even if you don't meet the buyers—which you may or may not want to do, for reasons you'll see shortly—you'll at least know that some of the objects that your parents bought, preserved, looked at, and touched are circulating widely in the world. Even though your parents are gone, all these strangers are still valuing the decisions they made long ago.

So let's start looking at how to have the best possible selling experience, starting with garage sales.

Garage Sales: The Do-It-Yourself Approach

Lynda Hammond was rummaging through the items at an older woman's garage sale near Phoenix when she came across a collection of antique clothes irons.

Hammond, a former TV news anchor who still has a love for listening to people's stories, had to learn more. "She grew up with 13 brothers and sisters. Her mother would wake up at 4:00 a.m., and every morning until 6:00 a.m., she'd iron clothing. It was a beautiful way for this woman to start her day quietly. It was a soothing, therapeutic time for her, since at 6, the kids would wake up and all hell would break loose."

Clearly, the irons were a treasure that helped this woman

Real-World Downsizing Discovery

Beth says: When my parents moved to assisted living and later passed away, I really wanted their dining room set. I had so many memories of family celebrations, baby and bridal showers, and graduations around that table. I could not let it go, but it never fit well in my house. A few years ago, I let a young family have it, and I bought a smaller set that I love and that fits the room and my taste. The memories were not in the furniture! I guess I thought it would help me hang on to my loved ones, but it was just stuff.

remember the care that her mother provided so long ago. I applaud her for letting them go when she no longer needed them, though I'm hoping that she kept the *best* iron that most strongly evoked these memories.

I also think she made the most of a terrific opportunity to share her mother's legacy with Hammond and the other shoppers that morning. Now, even you and I have "met" this mom as she quietly ironed before dawn, and her legacy lives on!

Hammond has turned her fascination with garage sales into a career through her Web site, GarageSaleGal.com. She offered some surprising ways to get the best return from your garage sale with the least hassle. No garage? This advice applies to yard sales, too.

Skip the price tag on your items. Traditionally, an early step in the garage sale process has been to buy a sheet of tiny stickers, write prices on them, and affix the stickers to your belongings. Don't, Hammond urges.

For one thing, those stickers cost money. They also take a lot of time to fill out. And the occasional unethical shopper may switch the price tags in order to take home an almost literal steal.

But the main reason not to price your goods is because the buyer might make a much better offer, Hammond says. "Let's say you decided you want to get rid of that 1940s sunflower-shaped cookie jar. So you'd take a dollar for it. Now let's say someone walks up and remembers the 1940s sunflower-shaped cookie jar that they broke when they were a child. This person might easily pay $30 for this, and you've undercut yourself!"

Sell on a day when you have less competition. Put your stuff out on Friday morning and be ready to welcome early visitors, Hammond suggests. "Most people think Saturday is the best day. It's not. The best day to have a garage sale is Friday," she insists.

That's because you'll tend to draw in shoppers who are on their way to work, or who are dropping kids off at school. You'll also get more garage-sale aficionados who have fewer other sales to visit since it's a Friday.

Hammond feels that you have a greater advantage in negotiating prices compared to selling on Saturday. That's because your buyers will assume that you're in no hurry to take a low price, since you can continue the sale another day.

Advertise it well. Let as many people as possible know that you're hosting the sale. She advises against newspaper classified ads, given their cost and the shrinking audience who reads them. It's free to put your advertisement on Craigslist, but this site tends to be crowded with garage sales, she says.

If you're on social media, post the date and time of your yard sale there. Consider posting a few photos of particularly interesting pieces to help bring in shoppers. You can also easily find Web sites that run garage sale ads (including Hammond's site).

Use simple signs. Put up signs in your neighborhood that direct shoppers to your sale. (If you're hanging them from trees, telephone poles, signs, fences, and similar locations, first make sure it's okay.) Be sure to remove them after the sale!

Use fluorescent poster board to make your signs. It doesn't matter which conspicuous color you pick—pink, yellow, green, or orange—but stick with the same color for all your signs, Hammond says. This gives your shoppers an easy-to-follow trail of clues to your home. Make the signs 15 inches square—anything bigger and they'll flap in the wind and may fall off.

Finally, just put the word SALE on your sign, with an arrow pointing in the correct direction. You don't need to clutter it with your address or phone number, she says.

Pretend you're running a store. This is another point in your family downsizing when you have to be businesslike. On this day, your garage is a retail environment, and you're the manager, Hammond says. Sweep the floor and provide good lighting. Have soft music playing in the background and make water, coffee, and lemonade available. (It's okay to charge for it.)

Make your merchandise look appealing, she urges. Dust it off. Group like items together, such as electronics and kitchenware. If possible, hang your clothing from racks so shoppers can browse easily.

Use a team. If possible, have at least four people working your garage sale, Hammond recommends. This is a good time to recruit any family members who'll be benefiting from the profits of the sale. Having assistants helps ensure that someone is available to answer questions, negotiate prices, and take payments. You'll also want someone to go out periodically to make sure your brightly colored signs are all still up and pointing in the proper direction.

Stay safety conscious. Keep all the doors to your home locked. Keep only a small amount of money outside for making change and stow it in a fanny pack on your waist. As more money comes in from customers, periodically take it inside and stash it in a safe place.

Sometimes customers walk off with merchandise without

paying. This is an unpleasant, but not uncommon situation at garage sales. If you see it happen, let it go, Hammond urges. Your safety is more valuable than the item.

Estate Sales: Bringing In a Professional to Bring In Shoppers

You might think of an estate sale as a bigger, more formal version of a garage sale that's typically held in the home that you're downsizing, though sometimes an estate sale company can sell the goods in another location. The public, which may wait in line to enter the home, walks around and shops. Sometimes items are marked with a price, and sometimes shoppers place their own bids.

Estate sales aren't for every downsizer. Before deciding to host one, it's important to set realistic goals, do some advanced work, and pick an estate sale professional carefully, Hall warns. Here's how.

Figure out if an estate sale is a good fit for your needs. How much stuff do you want to sell? Some estate sale professionals will only work with you if the sale is expected to bring in at least $5,000, Hall says. Others require an even higher minimum.

Ask yourself whether buyers will be interested in the stuff you're selling. Ideally, Hall says, sellers can offer a mix of big-ticket items and unique smaller collectibles to entice a diverse crowd.

Also, is your parents' home an ideal setting for a sale? A neighborhood association may not want hundreds of cars parked in the street during the sale. A high-rise apartment building may also frown on the foot traffic heading to a sale. On the other hand, is the home located far out in the country? People might not be willing to make the drive.

Understand what an estate sale company does. "Do not let Aunt Bessie's son's neighbor do it because he dabbles in antiques," Hall warns. A good estate sale professional must use a variety of skills in order to make your sale as successful as possible. Look for someone who can either accurately appraise your goods or call upon a network of contacts to provide this crucial service.

You'll also want someone with a proven ability to advertise your sale to the right shoppers so it brings them in like a "giant magnet," Hall says.

Do your homework on the estate professional. To find candidates who can run your estate sale, ask for references from people like your friends, your real estate agent, your lawyer, and your accountant. Interview at least three candidates before making your choice, Hall suggests.

Pay attention to these factors: Do they have a professional-looking Web site? Do they show up on time for the interview? Do they seem responsible and knowledgeable? Considering the reason why you're holding this sale, you'll probably want someone who also seems understanding and empathetic.

You can get a sense of their reputation by checking their references, the Better Business Bureau, and Angie's List, Hall says. It's also a good idea to visit a few of their sales and ask clients afterward about their experiences.

Be ready for the estate sale company to share in the profits. Expect for the company to charge 35 percent of what you bring in. You may also have to pay up-front consulting fees. When you're interviewing candidates, keep in mind that a more experienced (and expensive) company may more than make up for their fee by pricing your items more accurately and bringing in more shoppers, she says.

Consider making the sale a nonfamily event. I understand the appeal of wanting to hang around during the estate sale. It can be nice to get a sense of the people who will be providing a new home for your parents' possessions. Maybe you'd also like to tell them how much your parents enjoyed these items, but that can feel off-putting to estate sale buyers. The estate professional may not like having extra guests, either, Hall says. That's because family members have a tendency to disrupt the carefully planned sales environment. She's heard of a family member telling a shopper that "Aunt Sally died in that chair!"

During the sale, perhaps your family should go somewhere for a nice lunch or converge on a sibling's house to watch old home movies.

Sell Your Stuff Online

There's a lot to be said about turning to the Internet to unload your parents' stuff. For starters, you can connect with three billion potential shoppers around the world. You also have access to popular sites that make it relatively easy to reach these people—like Amazon, Craigslist, and eBay—and many lesser-known sites to help you sell specific items like electronics and clothes.

Note that I said *relatively* easy. Selling your parents' stuff online can still be challenging, especially if you're in a hurry to finish downsizing their home. You're competing with a lot of other sellers, so you'll need to have interesting offerings, and you'll need to cleverly market them at a good price. You also must know the ins and outs of how these sites work, and you'll need to know how to interact safely with the spectrum of unique people you'll encounter online, including scammers.

Each site has its own rules and customs. I'd recommend that you do some research online for the sites that best meet your needs (for example, how much will you have to pay the site? How convenient is it to use? Will you need to meet the buyer in person or will you have to mail the items?).

Wherever you choose to sell your parents' household items, keep these general ideas in mind.

Find the right price. Look online for the typical price that other people are setting for similar items, and list yours comparably. Also, try to get a sense of how many of these things are available in retail stores and on the used market.

If they're easy to obtain, that's probably going to lower your asking price. But if you suspect that you have an uncommon item or it seems to be in especially good condition, this is evidence that likely supports a higher asking price.

Describe the item well. When you write the title and description for the item, use keywords that will bring up the listing when shoppers search for it. If they can't find it, they can't buy it! If you were looking for this thing, what words would *you* put in the search box?

Also, use lively writing to make the item sound appealing (think like an advertiser or marketer would), but accurately describe the item. If it has damaged spots or flaws, acknowledge them, too. Finally, use good grammar and spelling. This gives you the air of a well-informed seller, and it makes your wares more attractive.

Take great pictures. The photo you include of the item can make shoppers reach for their credit cards or run the other way. So take time to make it good. Be sure the item is clean and free of dust. If possible, shoot the photo in natural light (in other words, sunlight) and place the object against a noncluttered, plain background.

Be sure that you're close enough to capture details of the object that will interest the buyer. If it's large, you might want to post a close-up or two alongside a photo of the entire thing.

Respond to user questions. When you walk into a retail store and can't find any employees to answer your questions, how likely are you to make a purchase? The same is true when you offer items for sale online. Your potential buyers are probably going to want to ask for more details about your item. So regularly check for messages so you can answer these questions promptly.

STEP 9: DONATE REMAINING ITEMS

You're very close to being finished with your downsizing project. If you have items of value that you couldn't sell at a garage sale, estate sale, or online—or you decided not to bother trying to sell them—it's time to donate them to charity.

Your parents brought these items into their home because they saw some type of value in them. I set up the *Let It Go* process to help you honor your parents' legacy as much as possible. You now have the opportunity to help your parents' choices continue to make a difference for a lot of people.

Their remaining I-Might-Need-It Items can provide a fun moment for a kid who wouldn't otherwise have it, clothes for an unemployed person who wants to make a good impression at a job interview, appliances to parents starting over after a crisis, or just a bit of joy to people who love bargains. These items also support jobs for the people who process and handle them.

In return, your family may be able to deduct the value of the goods you donate at tax time. When possible, get a receipt from the organization listing the date of the donation and the items you gave. Talk to your tax professional—or check out the IRS Web site—to learn more about how this process works.

You can check out groups in your area that accept household items at CharityNavigator.org.

As you select items to donate, ask yourself: *"Would I feel good about giving this toy to my child in its present state? Would I feel good about my guests sitting on this couch? Does this blender have a lid, and does it turn on when I plug it in?"*

If the answer is no, then don't pass it along to the charitable organization. The more trash they have to sort out, the more work they must pay someone to do.

That said, some will sell overly worn or stained clothing to recyclers. If you're uncertain whether your items will be useful, call and ask! Also, if the organization sends out a truck to pick up your goods, make sure to set them out on time so the hauler doesn't waste a trip.

STEP 10: DISPOSE OF TRASH

Congratulations—you've reached the end of your downsizing! But even at the finish line, you still have a bit of important work to do to ensure that your parents' downsizing is as meaningful and sustainable as it can be, with as little waste as possible.

To the extent that your community makes it feasible, please recycle as much of your trash as you can. Take hazardous items (like household chemicals, old batteries, cans of paint) to the approved drop-off site in your area, or ask your trash service about options it can offer for these items.

Also, make use of the many options you have to recycle unwanted electronic devices. Again, your community may offer a drop-off point for these items. Some big-box electronics and office-supply stores will also accept these devices and some other household appliances. For recycling sites available in your area, check out GreenerGadgets.org.

Just make sure that the organization you plan to use will accept the specific items you want to recycle. (In some cases, you may have to pay a fee.) Also, even if the organization says it will wipe the data off an old computer, tablet, or other device, it's wise to do this yourself before you drop it off.

Hopefully, after you've repeatedly sifted through your parents' "material convoy" with each of these steps, all you're left with is stuff that really, truly has nowhere else to go but the landfill.

Bag it up and set it out in the appropriate place for your trash collector to take it.

You can now consider your parents' home thoroughly and completely downsized in the *Let It Go* manner. You've made it through one of the more significant family experiences a son or daughter will have.

I hope the process draws you and your family together, and that everyone comes away with the elements you'll need for a healthy sense of closure. May you carry only the memories and stories of your parents that bring you happiness, and create new ones to treasure with the loved ones who remain.

AFTERWORD

Just 6 weeks after moving out of her home of 31 years, Susan Moore sounded like a different person. In a sense, I suppose she was, given that she'd gotten past the biggest change in her adult life.

She was finally living in the same town as her grandchildren. Between jobs at the moment, she was getting a taste of retirement a decade early. But part of her noticeable lightness also seemed to come from her new mindset about her possessions.

As you may remember from Susan's story in Chapter 1, the weeks leading up to her move from the San Francisco Bay area to Arizona felt traumatic. Though her new home was actually bigger, the size of the Moores' moving trucks determined how much they could take.

At the time, letting her stuff go felt like "I was throwing away my life! It's like you're committing suicide if you throw away your life!" she said.

Because she filled the trucks with stuff she didn't truly want, she had to leave behind some items she actually needed. Her electric grill and some other worthy kitchen items went to a donation center. When she pulled away in her car, the pile she left on her curb as trash held a number of useful belongings, including two bowling balls in their bags.

She couldn't put a value on the useful items that she could have sold or that she had to replace after she arrived at her new house. "It was probably a lot! More than a dinner out, I can tell you that!" she says. "Actually, I just bought a bowling ball this week because I'm bowling with my parents."

Many of the things she brought, on the other hand, felt unnecessary in her new life.

"I packed things I found in the shed that my kids used to play with. I thought, 'I'm going to play with those with my grand-children.' But I have brought them out a few times, and they have no interest! My 2-year-old grandson is an expert on the iPad. We've been doing numbers games, and he knows all his shapes, just from doing these games. He doesn't care about the Mr. Potato Head that I had from when my son was little."

On the day of this follow-up conversation, Susan was plan-ning on picking out some of her treasures (like putting her daughter's baby shoes and an outfit into a shadow box to honor them), then selling a lot of her unnecessary stuff at an upcoming community garage sale.

"The first time you start letting go of your stuff, it hurts. But I'm still me. My life is even better. I don't need all that stuff in the bins that I thought I needed," she says. "If I knew someone going through the downsizing process right now, I swear I'd go to their house and help them. I can honestly tell you . . . you think you need your junk, but look at this stuff! You don't need it! It doesn't fit in with your new life."

Now that you've reached a new phase in your own life, I hope you've surrounded yourself with only the treasures that bring back satisfying and uplifting memories and the worthy items that help you function at your best.

I also hope that your downsizing-related milestone hasn't left you feeling a little empty or numb, or full of doubts and what-ifs about the choices you've made.

But if it has, you're certainly not the first downsizer to feel that way.

IT'S HUMAN NATURE FOR BIG CHANGES TO BRING CONFLICTED FEELINGS

Recently, I was talking with a friend of mine, Jay Edwards, MA, MFT, about how downsizing-related changes affect us. As a marriage and family therapist, he noted that "I work with a lot of people who say 'I don't understand! I made this move, I have this new job, or I moved to this new city, which is what I've always wanted, but I just feel sad or melancholy or anxious.'"

If you're having those feelings, it's for reasons that can be explained. For starters, Edwards says, we tend to organize things as either/or: They're either right or wrong or good or bad. This helps us make the world around us seem more understandable. But this outlook can make life changes feel confusing.

That's because life isn't really either/or, especially when it comes to change. Sometimes you'll feel one type of emotion *and* a conflicting one at the same time!

For example, some people need lots of thrills and new experiences. Picture the adrenaline junkies, adventurers, and world travelers in this group. On the other hand, some people crave consistency. They eat at the same restaurant every Wednesday night for 30 years, he says.

But "for most of us, it's somewhere in the middle. Those two impulses are fairly equally matched. When change comes—either contemplated and strategically planned out, or thrust upon us from an unfortunate event like divorce or death in our family— that equilibrium of two forces is thrown off-balance," he says. "It's going to be upsetting to the equilibrium of our psyches."

In addition, if you try to push away your painful emotion—"*I put money into a 401(k) plan for three decades to enjoy this retirement, and I'm just going to stop this silly grieving about my career being over*"—it has the power to shove back. Try to ignore it, and it calls harder for your attention.

"When we try not to look at sadness, grief, anger, or disappointment because we only want to enjoy the good part of change, not only will we fail but, usually, we'll get knocked on our butts. That force is pushing back as vigilantly as we push against it," Edwards says.

So if you're second-guessing a well-planned decision that filled you with anticipation not long ago, that's perfectly understandable. If you're surrounded by fantastic new opportunities but keep focusing on the elements of your old life that are gone, that's not uncommon, either.

It doesn't mean you've made the wrong choice. It doesn't mean that you're an ungrateful person for feeling conflicted. It just means that you made a change, and afterward, it may take longer to sort through your emotions than it does for you to unpack your moving boxes.

SO NOW WHAT?

Your surroundings, and the activities you do in them, help create your identity. They give your life a particular structure, a bit like a dam that reshapes a river into a lake.

When your old surroundings disappear, or you stop doing certain activities, you may become like the flow of water seeking a new path after the dam collapses.

Who are you now? How should you use your time? What structures should you seek to provide a shape and direction that gives your life meaning?

People often ask themselves these questions after they stop smoking or break some other addiction. So do many caregivers after their loved one dies and they find themselves with empty hours to fill.

You don't have to find the answers to these questions right now. But today is a good time to start searching for them.

One way is to "open the door" and invite in your regrets and second-guesses for a closer inspection, Edwards says. (Or, to stick with the analogies throughout this book, dig deep until you find them, then pull them out and reframe them.)

Have you downsized from the house where you raised your family and now you're wishing you'd had another baby so you'd still have a child who needed daily mothering? Maybe this is actually indicating that you have a need to be maternal in some other way, he says. Maybe you could address these feelings by caring for, educating, or tending to fellow humans who *aren't* your children.

If you've finally retired, maybe the yearning you feel for your old desk is more about a need to be part of a team or to have the sense that your ideas are making a difference. Perhaps you could get the same fulfillment by volunteering at a local organization as a worker or leader, Edwards says.

If your downsizing has left you with time to fill or a need to redefine your identity, I would also strongly recommend volunteering. Even if your downsizing milestone doesn't put you in this situation—if you relocated for a new job, you might be busy, and if you just began a marriage, it has added to your identity—I'd still recommend devoting some time to helping others regularly.

As you've learned, you are not your stuff. Treasures hold some of your memories, and your worthy objects say a little about the things you do, but you are so much more.

Still, you can think even bigger. There's a lot more going on beyond the walls of your home or the structures that form the boundaries of your life. There are people you haven't met who could make your life richer. There are problems in your community that are waiting for you to help provide a solution.

The two cardboard boxes that my sister and I held outside the nursing home didn't really hold the sum of our mother's life. A box can't hold *yours* either, even a box the size of your home.

Now that you're in this new phase of your life, keep having experiences that are worth treasuring forever. Whether you're closer to 40 or 80, let your time and energy be worthy possessions that you use every day to improve your family, your neighborhood, or even beyond.

My hope for you is that as you cultivate new memories, relationships, and structures in your life, you'll hang on to the ones that make your heart sing. When you go through another big change in your life, and you will indeed, carry these with you.

All the rest that you encounter—the parts that make you feel bad, the clutter that blocks the doors to somewhere better, the obstacles that hold you back—get rid of them. Let yourself go forward to somewhere better.

ACKNOWLEDGMENTS

Letting go is never easy, yet it's something we all have to do constantly throughout our lives. For me, moving to the United States many years ago was the first experience of letting go and jumping into the unknown. Since then, there have been many times when saying yes to an opportunity (when often I only wanted to say no!) brought rewards that I could never have imagined. This book is borne out of those experiences, as well as the thousands of interactions I've had with people who struggled with the challenge of downsizing, either by choice or through circumstances forced upon them.

I know it's a cliché, but the truth is that no book writes itself. *Let It Go* is no exception. You may have noticed that I dedicated *Let It Go* to my family and friends, without whom this book would never have been written.

First and foremost to my husband and closest friend, Ken: My name may be on the cover of this book, but it's his love, support, enthusiasm, and encouragement that make it all possible.

To my mother and siblings, thank you. Family has always been so important to me, even more so since my mother passed away less than 12 months ago. Her passing was the impetus for *Let It Go*, and the process that my brothers, sisters, and I went through following her death played a key part in what you hold in your hands.

My closest friends—who are my adopted family—are also in these pages. Living so far from my family and home country,

I rely on them enormously, and they never let me down. For their friendship, support, good humor, and feedback, I thank them.

To my collaborator and wonderfully skilled wordsmith Eric Metcalf, I owe a huge thank you. This is our second collaboration and one that I've enjoyed enormously. It is a huge pleasure to work with such a talented writer and gifted storyteller. Let's do it again!

My editor at Rodale, Marisa Vigilante, has championed *Let It Go* from the start and provided valuable feedback and insights that have only improved the final manuscript. And to the creative and marketing departments at Rodale, thanks for making *Let It Go* look good and for promoting it so enthusiastically.

To the experts who so generously agreed to be interviewed for *Let It Go*—Brian Caverly; Carolyn Curasi, PhD; Jay Edwards, MA, MFT; David J. Ekerdt, PhD; Sam Gosling, PhD; Julie Hall; Lynda Hammond; Larry Lehmann; and Jennifer Lodi-Smith, PhD—thank you for sharing your perspective, your insights, and your knowledge. The book is richer for your contribution.

To those who shared their stories and anecdotes—Karen Cadman, Debra Clements, Meg Lightbown, Nancy Little, Susan Moore, Donna Vickroy, and many others—thank you. When it comes to letting go, we each have a story to tell and something to teach. Thanks to all of you for being so open and generous in telling your tale and shedding light on the process of downsizing.

And finally, to the many thousands of you who have supported my work and have responded so enthusiastically to the idea of decluttering and downsizing, none of this would have been possible without you.

I have seen that the stuff that comes into our lives—especially the belongings we inherit from those we love—can be a crushing burden. It's through the process of downsizing that we can find a path to personal freedom and the exciting opportunities that life has to offer. Jump on board, and enjoy the ride!

INDEX